Reality Check

The Challenges and Triumphs of
B.J. MacPherson's Life and Last Day on Ice

Rich Flammer

*"The basic difference between an ordinary man and a warrior
is that a warrior takes everything as a challenge, and an
ordinary man takes everything as a blessing or a curse."*
~ Carlos Casteneda, The Wheel of Time

Chapter 1 - The End

It was a three on two. San Diego Gulls' B.J. MacPherson, Tim Lovell, and Daniel Shank raced down the ice, working the puck towards the Idaho Steelheads goal. Friday night. May 4th, 2001. The Bank of America Centre in Boise was sold out and packed with thousands of screaming hockey fans, most of them for Idaho. They came to watch game four of the Taylor Cup, the West Coast Hockey League's championship series.

This was B.J.'s fifth year playing for San Diego, third season as team captain, and fourth Taylor Cup Championship. The 27-year-old, 6'2" center was still in his prime, and led them to wins in two of the other three cups. This one, however, wasn't looking so good for the Gulls. They played the first two games at home, and lost them both. Then they went to Idaho, and barely won the third in overtime. In B.J.'s estimation, the Gulls were outplaying them, but the Steelheads' goalie was standing on his head. And Idaho's entire team was tough... By far San Diego's fiercest rivals in the league.

Both the Gulls and Steelheads signed key players at the deadline before the playoffs, a common practice in AA minor pro hockey. San Diego got Lovell and Shank this way. Going into the series, B.J. knew it was going to be a battle, but the Gulls at the time were one of the best teams he's ever played on. The right blend of speed and physical presence. Their second and third lines were as sharp as their first, but this was also true with the

Steelheads, who shared domination of the WCHL's entire season with San Diego's Blue and Orange.

Everyone on the ice was playing full-tilt. B.J. remembers, "It was easily the toughest series of games I've ever played, making me wanting the championship that much more." A veteran iceman who backed up his words with hard work and grit, B.J. went into battle for the team with selfless dedication, ready to fight, muck, give and take whatever pounding was necessary for the win. His energy level set the pace on the ice, and pumped up his teammates.

To add to the intensity of the match-up, Idaho's coach, John Olver, and the Gulls' Steve "Marty" Martinson, were long-time, bitter adversaries. Martinson and Olver had met in the Taylor Cup finals three times before this series, with Marty prevailing twice.

Both had received multiple West Coast Hockey League (WCHL) coach of the year awards, and when they shared coaching responsibilities at a league all-star game a couple of years prior, they couldn't have stood further apart behind the bench, not speaking a word to each other. Their animosity was well known by fans, players, and the media. "He doesn't like me, and I don't like him," Marty once summed it up bluntly to an Idaho reporter.

Unlike professional football or baseball, hockey players must endure a seemingly endless string of playoff battles in pursuit of a title. Multiple rounds have to be won to advance, with each game of every series equally critical, as well as physically demanding.

Injuries come easily in a game where exceptionally fit, amped athletes carry weapons, swinging and poking sticks at each other, the confined space of the rink often leaving little room to avoid an unwitting encounter with a puck cutting through the air at speeds of up to one hundred miles per hour, bone rattling hits coming continuously, often without warning, from all angles and directions. The brief rest in between games allows little time for wounds to heal, and players wince through the pain as they slug it out night after night, with only adrenalin and cortisone to temporarily mask their stings.

For a player like B.J., who relished every moment on the ice and the privilege he felt to be paid to play hockey, the aches and pains were little more than paper cuts to an accountant. At first a sting of pain, but quickly overshadowed by the prevailing task at hand. End the day with the numbers on your side, and nothing else is remembered.

Idaho's rink had already been covered in plastic fish, the fans' traditional way of acknowledging their team's first goal of games played on home ice, and the Steelheads pleased the crowd by adding two more. The Gulls were down by three and continued scoreless for nearly fifteen minutes of the second period, when they finally had a good opportunity to get on the board. The Steelheads got caught with three men deep in San Diego's defensive zone, opening a breakout play for B.J. and his adept offensive line.

Skating backwards, Idaho defenseman Adam Borzecki tried to keep up with B.J. in the neutral zone, but realizing the Gulls' center was going to pass him, turned to go forward. As Borzecki spun around off balance, B.J. got a fist full of his jersey, tugged him down at the blue line, and skated past him.

Now it was a three on one, and Lovell passed the puck to Shank, who fired a shot. Idaho's goalie Chad Alban made the save, but the puck remained loose, and B.J. put the brakes on hard to the right of the net going for the rebound, a cloud of ice splayed into the air by the sharpened edges of stainless steel.

As he contorted his body to get his stick on the puck, B.J.'s feet came out from underneath him, and the athletic attempt to jam one past Idaho's netminder landed him on his back, sliding uncontrollably towards an inconceivable fate. When he stopped, he remained in that awkward position for only a second or two, but it was long enough to end his life as a hockey player.

Borzecki caught up to the action in the Gulls' attacking zone, half-heartedly poked at the puck, but seemingly was more interested in the opportunity to exact a little revenge on the opponent that had just muscled past him and threw his butt on the ice. In a blind rage months after the incident occurred, B.J. blistered: "I knew after I pulled him down, there was only one thing on his mind. He didn't even fuckin' *care* about the puck, wasn't trying to clear it out of the crease. He was going right for me. He was coming to hurt me."

At a speed fast enough to make it count, the rough, Polish-born defender aimed his large body at the Gull's fallen leader, and forced a well-padded knee and his 220-pound frame directly onto the forward crown of B.J.'s head. As the puck remained loose for a moment, Borzecki put a little icing on the cake by repeatedly jamming his thick leather glove into B.J.'s face, which, at this point, was already wincing in excruciating pain. The face wash was an act both B.J. and his mom would later forgive Borzecki for. "That's hockey," his mom Peg told doctors who began to express disgust as they watched the leather facial B.J. received on tape. "The hit, well that's a different story."

The Gull's bench boss, however, about as tough as they come, was less forgiving. "B.J.'s lying there defenseless on the ice, and he punched him." A rugged player who had over 3,000 penalty minutes in 628 career games, including stints with three NHL teams, and a record of 49 major penalties in the American Hockey League that still holds, Marty Martinson knew a few things about hits.

No one will ever know if more damage to B.J.'s spine came from the face smack. And while that may have been pardoned, there was no tolerance in B.J.'s mind for the initial blow. "When I was growing up in Canada," he recalls, "our hockey coaches used to show us a movie every year about cheap shots. Hitting from behind... It's the worst thing you can do." Cheap shots are particularly sinister in the power they possess to severely injure the player on the receiving end, even if the intention of the player administering the blow was less benign.

The puck never went in, the clock stopped at 5:44, and B.J. remained prone in the slush next to the crease. The refs and some players from both teams hovered around him for a few moments, as his muddled gaze was inadvertently fixed heavenward. "Get Billy, I can't feel anything," B.J. says to Daniel Shank. "C'mon, I'm not joking. This is serious."

His words, and perhaps the starry look in his eyes, prompted his teammate to quickly motion over Gulls' head athletic trainer, Billy Taylor. Immediately recognizing the severity of B.J.'s condition, Taylor huddled over him, as the mood in the arena quickly turned from rowdy and loud to somber, hushed and gray.

Hockey fans love a good hit, especially when it's one of their own delivering the blow... the distinctive sound of bodies covered in plastic pads cracking against the boards and each other resonating through the chilled arena air.

But this collision was less dramatic than most. Most of the crowd didn't even see it happen. No noise from the contact even made it to the seats. No "crack" or "thwack" as is commonly heard from direct hits echoed through the rink. No low-pitched "thump" of a body stuffed into the boards, no typical building filling sound that makes people gyrate suddenly from their popcorn, loved one or beer to see what the hell just happened down there on the ice.

While some may say many of the people filling the seats of the arena are there for, or at least enjoy the macabre, there's definitely a limit to the fans' delight when it comes to hockey bell ringers. Although there are plenty of smashes, crashes, and occasional injury-inducing hits in a game - some staining the ice with blood - it's not often a player down will muffle the crowd's cheers.

But even *they* know sometimes. When it's one of those hits or collisions or slashes that go slightly beyond the already intensive physicality of the game. They can *feel* it. When chaotic screaming is replaced with silence, and rabid, bloodthirsty hockey fans temporarily return to being human, overheard mumbling to each other in lowered, concerned voices, "Holy shit, this guy is *really* hurt. I mean, he's on the other team and all, and that was a great hit, but I hope he's okay. *Fuck... this looks really bad...*"

B.J.'s girlfriend Angela was listening to a radio broadcast of the game from her apartment, more than seven hundred miles to the south in the Ocean Beach community of San Diego, California. At first she only knew a Gull was injured, which was enough to raise her pulse and bring her down. But then she learned it was her boyfriend.

And then she heard he wasn't getting up on his own.
More than 1,800 miles to the east and a bit north, a good half a continent away, B.J.'s mom Peg, who couldn't listen to or hear the game, looked at a clock on the wall of her Toronto home and simply thought, *It must be the second period by now.*

About half an hour later, she would get a call straight out of a hockey mother's worst nightmare.

B.J. lay motionless on the ice, in shock, and optimistically thinking it was merely a "stinger," a bone jarring hit that would wear off in a few minutes and allow him to get up on his own and resume play. Taylor's face was so close to his, he tried to push him away, but his limbs wouldn't respond.

Then his right arm rose and fell to the ice, and from the corner of his eye, B.J. watched it go without having the ability to stop it. When you see the replay you can see this action transpire. It was as if B.J.'s head was fixed to the ice straight up and couldn't move, and his eyes caught a glimpse of some activity happening and rolled towards it. That activity was his arm, but...

"I didn't even *lift* it myself. I just watched it move without *feeling* it move. It was fucking eerie."

They began cutting off his hockey sweater and gear, piece by piece, as Taylor held his head. B.J. had no idea how badly he was hurt. But his seasoned trainer did, and the man B.J. called "Mother Hen," due to an exceptionally maternal dedication to the well being of the players, most likely saved him from more extensive injuries, if more extensive injuries were possible at the time.

Taylor wouldn't let *anyone* touch B.J., as he lay immobile on the ice. The trainer sent for a neck brace and a backboard, with the board arriving first. An attending paramedic told Taylor to let go of B.J.'s head, but the trainer refused until he got the collar on the crippled player himself. Understandably upset, as he was the first of a select few people who truly understood the extent and magnitude of B.J.'s injuries, Taylor's concern was pivotal to B.J.'s recovery and survival. "The only reason I'd let go of his neck," he barked at the inexperienced paramedic, "is to strangle yours!"

Despite having lost all feeling from his neck down, B.J. was still thinking that maybe things weren't as bad as they seemed. "Maybe this is just the *mother* of all stingers," he was thinking.

Like one of those stifling hits that make the highlights on the evening news, sending an NFL player to the turf for a few minutes. But one they shake off and walk to the sidelines on their own from. "This *has* to be a stinger," B.J. told himself, having never experienced this sort of aftershock from a hit and unable to account for what he was feeling in any other way.

It wasn't a stinger. After 20 minutes, the equivalent in time of an entire period of hockey, he was strapped to a gurney like a couple of hundred pounds of lumber to a roof rack, and almost as equally stiff, lifeless and brittle.

Despite his tentative physical condition, the Gulls three-goal deficit weighed heavy on his mind.

As captain of the team, B.J.'s lead was powerful. Teammates respected how he played, what he said, and how hard he worked. He was the consummate gamer, willing to take one for the team, do *anything* it took to win. Excellent hockey skills and willingness to drop the gloves and go a few rounds with opponents also made him a fan favorite. He was a goal scorer who could fight, replete with finesse and brawn, and his good looks, quick wit and silver tongue enhanced his popularity. Off the ice, he partied with a passion, and to such a degree that Marty advised players not to join him in his nighttime misadventures. Not so much because the coach worried about B.J.'s performance the following day, but rather for some of the players who simply couldn't keep up, and were always rendered lethargic on the ice the morning after.

"Alright boys," Marty once said to the team. "You've got a day to fly. Anyone going out drinking, I don't want drinking with B.J. You're gonna get in trouble, never going to keep up with him, and he's a fucking asshole."

Impressed enough with B.J. as a hockey player to issue him his own number 28 when he joined the Gulls, the coach had different feelings for his captain's late night antics.

For the first time in B.J.'s hockey career, he had no control of what happened on the ice, nor his post game shenanigans. He suddenly had no control over the functions of his own body. He confessed to me one day that he had always felt invincible, like Superman. Ironically, one of the first people that came to his mind as he lay on the ice was Christopher Reeves.

The arena remained hushed. B.J. tried to stay positive, but it was becoming increasingly difficult to be optimistic. Mark Stitt held his hand, and as he was going through the Zamboni door, his head strapped to a board and fixed upright, he made eye contact with the Idaho fans. While the "boos" and jeers of away games always pumped him up, the concerned look Steelhead fans now had in their eyes had the opposite effect.

In a show of respect, they were *clapping* for him rather than heckling him. Although he appreciated the gesture, it spooked him more than anything else. The grimness of his injury reflected from their eyes, and he felt the gravity of his situation in the silence the arena had become. In B.J.'s words, "From the way they were looking at me, I could tell how fucked up I was."

It may sound trite, and a little too win-one-for-the-Gipperish, but as he was leaving the ice, B.J. told Mark, "Don't worry, I'll be okay. You tell the guys to go win this one for me." A highly unlikely and seemingly impossible task in hockey to come back and score four goals in the little over 25 minutes of play left on the clock. "You take care of yourself, we'll take care of the game," Mark replied, as his mangled friend and teammate was wheeled out of the arena, his condition worsening by the second.

One of the paramedics looked down at B.J.: "How ya doing?" When he tried to reply, his lips only quivered, and no words came out. At that moment, the limp, haggard player discovered the injuries he had sustained not only took away his ability to move his arms and legs, but also the power to contract his chest muscles enough to bring air to his lungs. *B.J. could no longer breathe.*

An emergency tracheotomy was necessary, so a slit was quickly made in his throat and a tube was inserted into his trachea to supply oxygen. B.J. tried to remain optimistic, but this event tested his will. "I *still* thought I was going to be okay, but when this happened, I remember thinking: 'Holy fuck! Now I'm not even breathing!'"

But it takes more than a stretcher to remove the presence of a warrior like B.J. from the ice. Someone who has dedicated his entire existence to the one thing in his life that made him feel whole, fully sentient and alive. His teammates didn't know just how bad his injuries were as they played on, but they knew an opponent had just taken out their captain, and understood how important that game was for him.

How well, or poorly, the team responded would reflect B.J.'s lead. His heart was so entirely in the game, and his condition so unimaginably wicked, the outcome of the series had the power to influence his recovery. In his mind, his life depended on it. And as tough as he was, in the ensuing weeks, he would need every fraction of inspiration he could find to survive.

As B.J. was leaving the arena in the body that moments earlier and years before dominated the ice - now completely numb and lifeless from the neck down - he wasn't even thinking about never being able to walk again.

He was dreading the possibility he'd never be able to *skate*.

Chapter 2 - The Beginning

The last time B.J. had been down on the ice for anywhere close to this long was when he was ten years old, playing hockey back home in Toronto. Near the end of the third period, one of the opposing players checked him hard enough to knock him off of his feet. He wasn't hurt, but he lay on the ice until the trainer came out. Why he did this is unknown, but he was a ten-year-old, and likely had some sort of reason in his own green mind to justify this action. When the game was over, he looked for his mom in the stands… but she wasn't there.

Now in the locker room, he took off his gear and put it in his hockey bag. Once dressed, he walked outside, but still couldn't find her, so he went to where he remembered she had parked the car. The engine was running, and his mom was sitting inside. She was fuming. Livid. Almost beyond mad to speak. "Boy, the next time you lay on the ice like that, you *better* be injured, or you're walking home!" She was dead serious, and they lived 45 minutes away.

B.J.'s dad, Billy MacPherson, was a coal miner from Nova Scotia. He lost a lung from his profession when he was 36. Just after he had returned from World War II, his brother Murray had a date with a girl named Peg. Apparently the date didn't go so well, because the next night Billy took her out. Their date went a bit better, and just three weeks later, Peg and Billy married. The marriage lasted months shy of 25 years, but Uncle Murray and Billy's relationship never quite recovered.

Billy was a guy with tons of heart. Growing up in a predominantly Catholic neighborhood, he was only five when he saw the local kids picking on Fred Snow, one of the few Protestants on the block. Billy didn't like that, and stuck up for him on sheer principle, wedging his already large frame and belief system between the aggressors and Fred. That simple, yet profound act led to the two becoming livelong best friends.

Nicknamed "Fish" for his inability to swim, Fred went to war with Billy, and when they returned, Fred also met the woman he wanted to marry, but tragically lost his wife-to-be on the very day they were to be married.

The MacPhersons willingly took him in the following day, and he's lived with them as family ever since.

An opinionated, outspoken personality had the family affectionately liken him to Archie Bunker, and Fred quickly gained another nickname, "Archie." This one stuck. Although he never married, the day he lost his fiancé, he gained an entire family. Sometimes the best gifts come in the ugliest packages, as the adage goes. Newer members of the MacPherson clan, such as B.J.'s nieces and nephews, have no idea who "Fred" or "Fish" is, but have incredibly fond feelings for their "Uncle Archie."

B.J. was the youngest of six, with two brothers and three sisters. They lived in Pelham Park Gardens, on the west side of Toronto, Canada, in a neighborhood known as "the Junction." Once a separate town, the Junction was annexed by the city in 1909. The place got its name from the intersection of four railway lines, and was the home of the Ontario Stockyards until 1993. One of the largest livestock markets in North America, the Junction earned Toronto its nickname, "Hogtown."

It was a rough area, with a lot of fights, and sometimes even full-on riots triggered by racial divides. Growing up in this sort of neighborhood gave B.J. an edge that would later prove invaluable to his career in hockey, as well as dealing with challenges like the life-threatening injuries commonplace in hockey.

One night his dad Billy went to the bus stop to walk Peg home. It was pouring rain. There was an African Canadian woman waiting alongside of her. With only one umbrella, Billy refused to get under it with Peg, getting soaked instead and letting his wife share it with this unknown woman. While it may not sound like much, that sort of thing just didn't happen in Pelham Park Gardens at the time. People just didn't cross racial divides, and when they did, it was usually to hurt somebody, not help them out. Billy never consciously *tried* to be, but he was an exception to the prevailing intolerance that jaded his neighborhood.

Years later, at Qualcomm Stadium in San Diego where the Chargers play, B.J. would be involved in a similar situation, his actions reflecting the same strength of character, whether inherited, or gleaned from, his dad.

The consummate sports fan, Billy had a head for statistics like no one else in the neighborhood, or quite possibly the entire region. Sometimes late at night, there'd be a heated argument somewhere in the suburbs of Toronto about a particular player or team's stats, and the phone would ring at the MacPherson's. "You're wrong," someone would bark. "Call Billy!"

In the days way before the Internet, there was little hope in such a search for an answer, which made Billy a true gem. Hockey, football, baseball... it didn't matter. He almost always could settle the dispute with his breadth of knowledge. B.J.'s sports acumen today rivals that of his dad's, and there are few major sports he couldn't expound the same expanse of knowledge upon.

Billy didn't make it to too many of B.J.'s games, but then again, B.J. hadn't had much of a career going yet at seven years old, when, sadly, his dad passed away. Billy may have left his son without a lot of attention, but B.J. got most of his size, his toughness, and most importantly, the best of his character and heart.

After B.J.'s dad died, Peg never went on another date again, and refused to sleep in their bed without him. Since his passing, she sleeps on the couch. At 6'4," Billy's frame was so big, and at 5'1," Peg's so small, she used to sleep propped up against him, like he was a human wall. The couch, she says, even though he's gone, "feels like Billy's still behind me." Even when she visits family or stays in a hotel, she insists on sleeping on the couch. Eccentric? Refusing to let go? No. Not at all. It's a beautiful, heartfelt, livelong homage to the man she loved.

~

The night B.J. was injured in Idaho playing hockey wasn't the first time he was taken to the hospital. When he was just two and a half years old, he fell off his bike and got five stitches in his hand. The next day, on his mom's birthday, he gave her a terrible gift. She was in the kitchen making him lunch. Pot steaming on the stove. He got on top of a garbage can to see what she was cooking, and the can started to wobble.

Peg grabbed him under the arms, but he was still wobbling uncontrollably, and for balance he grabbed the pot full of oil she was cooking French fries in. It dumped over his head, burning his face so badly he needed skin grafts. A French fry was stuck to his shirt, still so hot it was burning him right through the fabric. When his mom pulled the shirt over his head, it took a large piece of skin with it. His left ear was so burned and swollen, it hung down low enough to touch his shoulder. And his other burns were so severe, he was in the hospital for almost three months.

When B.J. was four, he was riding in a car with his oldest sister Louise and her boyfriend. They stopped short, and B.J. flew into

14

the windshield, cracking it with his head. He made it out of this incident okay, but felt so bad about the damage to the car, he offered to pay for it out of the measly number of coins in his piggy bank.

The next year, he chased a ball through a couple of parked buses into the street and got hit by a school van. With a fractured skull, he lost his memory for five days, and was unable to recognize anyone in his family.

Absent his dad, B.J.'s mom and sisters raised him, with the help of his brother Fred and the stalwart Uncle Archie. Sister Louise spent so much time with B.J., people joked about her being his mother.

Fred and Archie shared a room together, and both of them helped B.J. learn hockey. Fred played in an industrial league. B.J. remembers visiting him after his Sunday morning games, and between periods, seeing almost everybody on the team drinking beer and partying in a smoke filled locker room. Old school. Like B.J., Fred was a good hockey player, and as center, was particularly focused on and skilled at the face-off. Through hours of thoughtful instruction, he helped his younger brother master it as a science.

Uncle Archie helped B.J. learn the game as well. And he made sure there was plenty of opportunity for B.J. to hone his skills. Archie flooded the concrete courtyard in front of their house with a garden hose to create ice for B.J. and his friends to play on. And he often took B.J. to Brother Edmund Rice School as well, where the city built a large outdoor rink in a field.

Only a block away, Uncle Arch would lace up B.J.'s skates at home, and the fledgling player would walk right down the cement sidewalk with them on, trying to find little patches of ice so he wouldn't dull the blades.

At the outdoor rink at Edmund Rice there'd be 60 hockey players or more on the ice at the same time, all different ages and skill levels, playing a single game together. The action would begin with everyone dropping their sticks in the middle of the ice. One guy would pull his hat over his eyes, and go down the line flipping sticks back and forth.

Whichever side your blade pointed to, that was the team you were on. That's where B.J. *really* learned to play. If you could go end to end in that gong show with dozens of people on the ice chirping and jabbing at you, you were a hockey player.

On Saturdays and Sundays, B.J. would often spend twelve hours out there playing. The only reason he'd go home is because the lights would go off at 6 p.m., and bedtime was too near to wait for the city workers to leave. That's when one of the older kids would knock the lock off the light box with an axe, and flip the switch back on, allowing the game to resume, often going on late into the night.

While too young to stay after dark, B.J. improvised and made good use of his youth, dedication and profound love of the game during the window of time allotted a teenager. Many mornings, setting out before gray light and the day's first bird chirps, B.J. and Archie would get there at 5 a.m. Long before most people even got out of bed, they'd be there practicing. Archie would mind the net while B.J. took shots.

Absent his dad, Uncle Archie always kept an eye out for B.J.... sometimes literally. They'd be playing cards, Archie would have a few drinks in him, and if B.J. won a few hands, he'd lean across the table and say in his thick Nova Scotian accent, "Hey by, you cheatin' me?"

"I ain't cheatin' Uncle Arch..."

"By da Jesus I think yas are," he'd glare

And then he'd take out his glass eye and put it on the table.

"I'm gonna keep an eye on you!"

B.J. entertained many of his friends with his uncle's trick, but Archie tired of it long before B.J. did.

While he didn't have an easy childhood, B.J. has good memories. When he wasn't playing ice hockey, he was thinking about playing hockey. He played baseball and basketball too, but nothing compared. And even though he didn't realize it at the time, almost every major experience he had as a child prepared him for a life on the ice. His family was supportive and strong, but never spoiled him. His mom, sisters and brother are people of integrity, principle, and will. And they passed that on to B.J. just like his dad did.

One day B.J. came home after a neighborhood kid beat him up. He walked into the house crying. His mom didn't give him a hug and tell him everything was going to be okay. She told him to stop whining, and sent him right back out of the house saying, "Now don't come back home until you find that kid and make *him* cry."

Whether it was Louise, Sandy, or Peggy Ann, B.J.'s sisters would also send him back out into the neighborhood after losing a fight to give it another go with the guy. They were all preparing him for a life of hockey, and also of course, for all of the bumps and twists and inevitable misfortunes of *life* itself.

How to play, how to fight, how to win, how to survive... His family's support helped him last sixteen years as a professional hockey player, earn numerous championship rings, and gave him a foundation of strength and vitality from which he matured into a man replete with character, conviction, intelligence, a powerful work ethic, and a good sense of humor to boot. All of these qualities made B.J. the kind of guy you enjoyed hanging out with, liked to be on the same team with, and knew would always have your back.

But no family, however strong, and nothing in B.J.'s past or quiver of exceptional character traits could have possibly prepared him for that night in Idaho, when the word "fight" suddenly took on a dramatically more profound meaning.

Chapter 3 - Chaos

As Billy Taylor remained with the team, Gulls' assistant coach Martin St. Armour rode with B.J. to the hospital. In the ambulance, Martin was holding B.J.'s hand, and began to weep. That's when B.J. finally realized how bad his injury really was. "It's not often you see a hockey player cry, but when they're doing it for you, it's hard to take. That's when I *knew* I was done."

With the trach in his throat, B.J. was able to breath again, and talk. "Shit Martin, stop crying. You're gonna make *me* cry." He peppered the paramedics with questions. "This happens all the time, right?" "I'm gonna be okay, right?" "It's just a stinger, eh?"

As professionals, they chose not to comment on his condition to avoid instilling a gravity or hope that could impact his stability. But it was driving B.J. crazy. "We're almost at the hospital," was all they'd offer in reply, and as he kept asking questions, they wouldn't even look at him in the eye. B.J. continued with the grilling, pleading to understand the extent of his plight, and all he heard repeatedly was, "We're almost there…"

Fighting the feelings of hopelessness overwhelming him, B.J. directed his questioning to Martin. "This is nothing right? I'm gonna be okay… *right*?"

A physician attending the game, Dr. Calhoun, called his friend Dr. Zimmerman, a local neurosurgeon, at home. Zimmerman had just put his kids to bed, and normally would have turned in himself, but he had a funny feeling inside he couldn't quite describe, so he went to the kitchen to make something to eat. That's when he got the call. *"One of the visiting team's hockey players just sustained a spinal injury, and it looks bad."* Even though he wasn't on its staff at the time, Zimmerman put down the phone and rushed to Saint Alphonsus Regional Medical Center.

Once at the hospital, Martin dialed two numbers on his cell phone. One was for B.J. to give his mom the news. The other was to break up with Angela. In a moment of hopelessness and self-pity, he told her, "Go find someone who isn't a cripple."

B.J. only remembers pandemonium in the room they brought him into. There were lots of doctors and nurses rushing around, and it seemed to him like nobody really knew what to do. Then Zimmerman came in and took control. B.J recalls Zimmerman yelling something like, "Anyone not doing anything, get the fuck out of here!" This upset the staff doctor in charge, and a heated discussion took place. Then there was even a shoving match! A man who didn't even know B.J. was fighting for the hockey player's life.

Before Zimmerman showed up, B.J. was talking to his mom, with Martin holding the cell phone to his ear. A doctor came in and interrupted his conversation. "It doesn't look good son," he told B.J., but then said, "We still have to do X-rays." B.J. interpreted this as good news, and told his mom, "It's gonna be okay, because they haven't even done the X-rays yet." But even as he was telling Peg everything's fine, doubt kept quickly creeping back into his mind.

The doctor soon reappeared. B.J. again interrupts the conversation with his mom. "It's worse than I thought, son. You're never going to walk again." B.J.'s heart sinks, and he begins to cry. And then he wanted to punch out that doctor but he couldn't move his arms.

His vertebrae were so out of whack, the X-rays could have caused a seasoned doctor to wince and cringe. But it's the condition of the spinal cord that matters most, and with the loss of feeling from his neck down, it was obvious it was tweaked and being pinched by the misaligned bones. B.J., now heavily sedated, has people around him crying, doctors telling him he'll never again stand on his own, and has left the ice as captain of a team down 3-0 in the game, and 2-1 in a championship series. He couldn't help but feel he was going out a loser.

His prognosis was "flaccid paralysis of all four extremities, no motor function distal to the C4 vertebra, and dislocation of C4-5." B.J.'s skull and first four bones of his neck had been pulled forward, and the C4 vertebra ended up in front of the C5, pinching the spinal cord. In B.J.'s own words, "someone stuffed my head into my belly button and I couldn't move anything on my body but my mouth."

Not that he really had any say in the matter, but in the heat of Zimmerman's tryst with the staff physicians, B.J. yelled, "I want him. I want him!" With the first doctor telling him he was done for life and simply wanting to put him in traction, and Zimmerman's *let's operate and see if we can do something for this guy* approach, B.J.'s reaction was understandable.

B.J. also remembers Zimmerman being the first doctor who said something positive to him. "Son, don't worry. I'm going to take care of you." And after watching the doctor fight for the procedure he felt was best, B.J. was given the first few wisps of hope since the injury occurred. And besides being an experienced, highly skilled surgeon and truly a godsend for B.J., Dr. Christian G. Zimmerman was the only one in the room at the time who could look the fallen hockey player in the eye without crying.

B.J. was put on a Stryker bed, which allowed him to be turned over. Surgery began at about 10 p.m., and lasted about two and a half hours. As he hung upside down, and Zimmerman cut away

21

and fused his neck bones, the outcome of both his surgery and the championship game was unknown as B.J. remained suspended in an anesthetized sleep.

Chapter 4 - For the Love of Hockey

B.J. learned to walk when he was ten months old, and just eight months later was already skating on double-edged blades behind a chair for balance. When he was five his mom signed him up for his first league. As a tyke he loved practicing, but for the good part of a year he refused to come off the bench. His family would come to watch, and he'd just sit there when the coach called his line. Game after game he wouldn't go in.

While some mothers might scream in frustration at their son seemingly wasting their time and money, it was comical for B.J.'s mom, who would put her excited son and his gear in the car, drive him to the rink, see him all suited up and ready to go, only to watch him shake his head "no" every time the coach wanted to put him in. Peg laughed and shook her head and exhibited all of the patience and confidence and love for her son she maintains to this day.

After months of his nonsense, the time came when B.J. finally agreed to play. It felt pretty good to him, and after two minutes, when his line was coming off the ice, his coach shut the door and turned B.J. back around to play out the rest of the game. "You're going to make up for all those games you wouldn't play B.J.," he told him. But the fledgling hockey star didn't mind. That was music to his ears, because from that game on he never wanted to leave the ice.

That is, until the time they put him in the net. The coach rotated players in and out of this position. Goal was the *last* place B.J. wanted to be, and his performance reflected his lack of enthusiasm as a puck stopper. After the opposing team scored three goals on their first three shots against him, he threw the stick out towards center ice, took off his gloves, put them on top of the net, and turned towards his family in the stands with tears in his eyes. The goal was wide open, and his back was facing center ice while the puck was still in play! If that won't get a coach to pull you from the goalie position and never put you back, nothing will. It worked, and B.J. played offense from that day on.

Despite his childish antics, B.J. quickly fell in love with hockey. He was so excited about practice and playing, he would set the clocks in his house ahead to make sure his mom got him there early.

Not that she needed the help. She didn't even realize he was doing this until they arrived at the rink one morning to find an empty parking lot and an unlit building. They sat there for a few minutes and a car approached. It was a policeman. He pulled up next to them, and rolled down his window. "Do you mind me asking what you're doing here?" he quizzed Peg suspiciously.

"Hockey practice," she replied.

"At what time," the officer inquired.

"Six o'clock," said Peg

"It's only ten to four," the officer continued.
"No, it's… It was five thirty when we left. I thought it was about ten to six right now. At least according to the clocks in the house." Peg looked at her watch.

"Funny, even my watch says ten to six…" Then she looks at her son with a little fire burning in her eyes. B.J. had set all the clocks in the house two hours ahead. And her watch too, just in case the clocks didn't fool her. They were now two hours early for his practice! His mom wasn't laughing too hard at the time, but the cop got a good chuckle out of it and was nice enough to go over to the coffee shop, buy Peg a cup of tea and B.J. a hot chocolate. And because it was a bad area, he waited with them for nearly two hours until other hockey players and their families started showing up.

When B.J. was eleven he played for the Toronto Marlboros. This was an elite team, with a hockey program dating back to the 1800's, and athletes in those early days of the club competing in baseball, football, lacrosse and boxing, as well as hockey.

Named after a long line of English Noblemen, the Dukes of Marlborough, the team became the Marlboros, and then the "Marlies." On par with the Marlies' tradition and storied history, B.J. was on the roster of an amazing team, with many future professional players on it, including NHL stars Eric Lindros and Grant Marshall. They won every tournament they entered. These were some of the best days of his life, and from age eleven to thirteen, he was in heaven.

After two years with the Marlies, B.J. joined the Mississauga Reps. But after just a year with them, they cut him from the team. This was one of the worst days in his life. Although he was only fourteen, he was downtrodden and sure his hockey career was finished.

But the Mississauga Blackhawks quickly picked him up, and B.J. and teammate Billy Robinson had such a good year, the coach frequently left them on the ice for double shifts. He especially enjoyed beating the Reps, which they did on a regular basis. Then the Reps wanted him back, but he remained with the Blackhawks.

At age sixteen, he was drafted by the Oshawa Generals, packed his gear, and left his cherished home to play hockey. The Generals are one of the most successful junior hockey franchises in Canada, and the team has won a record thirteen Ontario Hockey League championships, and graduated 184 players to the NHL, including Bobby Orr and Eric Lindros. B.J. played alongside Jason Arnott as a General.

He moved in with Vince and Dorothy Busitil, who had a home on Thornton Street in Oshawa. The Busitil's were "billets," families who opened their home to junior hockey players to help soften the transition of moving to and living in other cities to play. Teams pay billets a stipend to house players, and also give them perks like season tickets.

The billet family gets the satisfaction of helping teenage boys like B.J. pursue their livelong dreams of professional hockey, and the fledgling player they accommodate receives home-cooked meals, a warm, familiar bed at night, and company of people who share the deep love of the game. The Busitils became B.J.'s second family, and he has exceptionally fond memories of his time with them.

Twelve years after signing with the Generals, he was still getting paid to play. He had already far exceeded the average two to three years most players last in professional hockey. But the truth is, he never even cared about getting paid. He was thankful for the opportunity to play, for any team, *anywhere*. He simply loved the game that much.

There's an expression common to hockey players that goes: "You get paid for practice, and the games you play for free." But B.J. would have gladly done it *all* for free, as long as he could be on the ice all day and have enough money to eat when he got home.

Think of something you love to do, like eating at your favorite restaurant, lounging on the couch all day reading, watching old movies, surfing, riding a bike, or playing poker with your friends. It could be anything. Just something you truly enjoy spending time doing. Now imagine getting paid to do that very thing. Actually doing what you truly love, whatever that may be, and earning money to do it, every day.

Would you haggle about the salary, if it were enough to live on? Of course not. Your response would be more like, "Wait a minute, let me get this straight. You're going to *pay* me to do this?" You only have to have one thing in your life you absolutely love to do to understand B.J.'s bliss. He loved playing hockey that much.

In 1992, when he was eighteen, B.J. waited anxiously at the Montreal Forum as the NHL draft process took place. Each organization had a table set-up on the ice, and the stands were filled with jittery, talented, nail-biting, hopeful hockey players like him.

His mom was with there, as was sister Louise, family friends Dan and Louise Harding, and of course, his billets Vince and Dorothy, who wouldn't dream of missing this moment.

Rated for the sixth round, B.J. was already full of anxiety, but his nervousness was compounded, as this was the same year the draft opened to Europeans, and the pool of eligible players had increased substantially. He recalls the first eight rows of seats being occupied by Europeans, and so many were drafted, by the last round the predominantly Canadian crowd began booing them and cheering for any player from Canada that was called, regardless if they knew who he was or not.

B.J. and his group of supporters waited patiently for hours. Hundreds of names were called, but his was not one of them. The draft was nearly over, and he noticed a reporter from Montreal interviewing players that he knew weren't selected. She slowly was making her way over to him, the pit in his stomach growing and emotional heaviness he felt spiking as it became evident he wasn't going to make the draft.

She was now interviewing him, and then the words he came to hear echoed through the forum over the loudspeaker. "B.J. MacPherson, Washington Capitals." He hugged the reporter, and ran down to the ice.

It's a day he'll never forget, because it was easily the best one in his life.

Chapter 5 - What's in a Game?

As B.J. was lying in the hospital the first night, a million thoughts rushed through his head. One moment he wanted to kill everybody on his "list," like the guy that did this to him, the doctor who told him he would never walk again, and the league officials who were supposed to suspend Borzecki from play that night but who instead chose to offset his suspension with a Gulls player's penalty. The next moment B.J. wanted to kill *himself.*

Then he felt a little better, telling himself he was going to make it, that everything was going to be okay. Then he felt bad again. *Kill that fucking guy. And him too!* He went back and forth like this for hours, unable to move or even feel the body attached to his head. The same body he depended on for his career as a hockey player. The only tool he ever knew how to use was useless, lifeless and gray.

He talked to his girlfriend Angela again. Imagine the sting she felt getting the play-by-play on the radio of her boyfriend being carted off the ice, and then getting a call from him telling her that they were over. He's glad she didn't listen to him.

At a time when their relationship could have fallen apart, when she could have given up, lost the guts it took to look at the mound of limp flesh that used to be her boyfriend, hours earlier a fit, handsome, well-paid professional athlete, silver-tongued, bright, confident, secure and animated, now a motionless lump with a bad attitude strapped to a bed with all sorts of tubes coming out of him, Angela responded in a way that surprised him.

There were few positive things that came out of B.J.'s injury. But the fact that it cemented the way Angela felt about him, and how he felt about her, during an early phase of their relationship when neither of them were entirely sure things would work out anyway, was a true blessing. Without a second thought, she jumped on a plane to Idaho and slept in his hospital room every night.

And she's stuck by him ever since, his injury already putting her through more "thick and thin" in a few months than most wives would experience in a lifetime. They were married on March 13, 2004, and she's as tough, colorful, driven, smart and likeable as her husband. These qualities never shown as brightly through as when he was at his worst. A further testament to her character.

As Dr. Zimmerman was preparing him for the operation, B.J. remembers wanting to punch out the other doctor. Whether it was true or not, B.J. didn't want to hear he'd never walk again, and wasn't buying the fact that nothing could be done for him.

It was as if his coach and teammates shook their heads as he was leaving the ice and said, "We're behind 3-0. Sure, it's only the second period, but it's *late* in the second period, we're going to lose the game, and there's nothing anyone can do about it." Bullshit. That's not the way B.J. learned to play hockey, or live his life, and he wasn't about to let a pessimistic doctor tell him he was down for the count when he still had lots of fight left in him.

Zimmerman, on the other hand, brought a spirit with him into the hospital room B.J. could relate to, and had the wherewithal to successfully convince the doctor in charge that surgery was both possible *and* necessary if the paralyzed athlete splayed about before them were to stand any chance of functioning again. B.J. wasn't feeling too good about anything at this time, and certainly wasn't thinking clearly, but he had faith in Dr. Zimmerman, and amongst his carnival of thoughts realized this surgeon represented his only chance at recovery, if not simple survival.

With the same focus, fastidiousness and passion B.J. played hockey, Zimmerman went to work at his calling of surgery, and successfully removed the paralyzed athlete's C4 vertebra, fusing together what was left of his spine with plates.

B.J. awoke about an hour after the procedure. It was 1:30 a.m. Through glazed eyes he saw that Billy Taylor was again at his side. Despite being upside down on the Stryker bed, when B.J.'s eyes opened, Billy's face was once again about a foot from his, as it had been what seemed like moments before when he was sprawled out on the ice.

The first thing B.J.'s cloudy mind thought of was the game, and with a ventilator tube stuffed so far down his throat it felt like it was touching his stomach, the Gulls captain attempted his first post surgery words. B.J. started to mumble as Billy tried to get closer to hear him, and then had to resort to reading the upside down hockey player's lips. But he most likely knew what B.J. was going to ask even before he tried.

"Did we win?"

In critical condition from a motionless body, B.J.'s eyes shifted and looked out over the side of his head in anticipation of the response. And in great testament to their dedication to B.J. and the team, not to mention their superior playing ability, the Gulls came back and beat the Steelheads 4-3!

Tears flooded B.J.'s eyes, streamed down his face, and his misery left him, at least for the moment. His teammates played with their hearts on their sleeves and won that game for *him!* It was true. The victory was like an infusion of blood, injected into the helpless captain at a time he felt like his heart had been ripped out, tossed on the ice, and he was lying there to die.

31

For the moment, he felt a renewed faith in the chances of his recovery. His spirit soared, but for not much longer than a blink.

Chapter 6 - Hockey Scars

The series was now tied two games to two. The Gulls had another game in Idaho before returning to San Diego. Nurses moved B.J.'s limp body into different positions and put pillows under him every half hour or so to prevent bedsores. Heavily sedated, he doesn't remember much, except seeing his mom, Angela, his best friend Darren, and his oldest sister Louise come into the room. His mom and sister flew down from Canada, Angela took the first flight she could get from San Diego, and Darren flew in from Orange County.

He hazily recalls it feeling good to have them there, but as soon as he saw them, he started to cry. As much as he wanted his loved ones with him, he hated them to see him in that condition. They all had seen him injured before, but this time he was nothing more than a heap of bones, skin, and meat with a couple of eyes peering out of it. He felt trapped inside his own body.

Barely able to talk, with a tracheal tube, all he really had left were his thoughts. And what he was thinking wasn't pleasant. Besides the stomach-turning prospect that his hockey-playing days were over, he was mentally wrestling with the horror of never being able to use his body again, being pushed around in a wheelchair with a respirator, and having people look down at him in pity. That's quite a dramatic change from life as a professional athlete. And a haunting prospect for an individual like B.J., whose physicality defined his being.

Even though there was nothing he could have done differently to prevent the injury from happening, he felt as if he let everyone down. Because of him, he thought, all of these people in the room, the people in his life whom he loved, were feeling bad, and that made him feel worse.

Of course, hockey is a physically demanding sport, and injuries are common. Many players have had some sort of injury end their career on ice.

Prior to his crippling injury in Idaho, B.J. considered himself "lucky to have never really been hurt." At various times in his career, he had his cheekbone broken, separated his left shoulder twice, dislocated it once, had two operations on it with one resulting in the removal of an inch of his clavicle, tore the peroneal tendon, or "sheath" of his right ankle, had a couple of teeth knocked out, broke his nose, and fractured several fingers. But that's just standard fare for a hockey player.

One of his shoulder injuries came late in the season of 1995-96. He had the whole off-season to recover, so he went back to Pelham Park Gardens and spent the most of the summer lying on the couch eating his mom's home cooking. Each day began with "What do you want for breakfast B.J.? Bacon and eggs, pancakes, or waffles... Err, okay. You're nodding yes. I'll just make you all three like I did yesterday." Lunch and dinner portions were as equally generous.

At the beginning of the next season, he signed with the Gulls. Even though he was a bit out of tune with the game, and 20 pounds overweight, he got called up to play with the Gulls' International Hockey League (IHL) affiliate, the Long Beach Ice Dogs. Out of all the minor pro leagues, the IHL was considered the closest to the NHL. The call came after only the second or third practice of the season with the Gulls, and the Ice Dogs put him right into a game with the Phoenix Roadrunners.

He didn't have a bad game, but the summer on the couch had rusted him. During one of his shifts on the ice, he checked one of Phoenix's finesse players so hard behind the net, the trainers had to come out and help him off. Roadrunners' rugged enforcer, Mike MacWilliam, who played half a dozen games with the

N.Y. Rangers the season before, and was a member of the IHL Turner Cup championship team in 1995-96, the Utah Grizzlies, wasn't too thrilled about this. Before the puck even dropped, he lasered a glance at one of B.J.'s linemates and said, "Prepare to die motherfucker!"

He had the wrong guy! But to prove how little a part of the team B.J. was, and also how intimidating MacWilliam could be, B.J.'s teammate replied, "What?! It wasn't *me*!"

Then MacWilliam figured out it was B.J. who was owed the pounding. B.J. won the face-off, the puck slid through a defender, and as the sluggish overweight Gull skated down the ice, he didn't think twice when he felt a tug on his shoulder. That's just how out of touch with the game he was. B.J. hadn't even noticed the Roadrunners made a line change and put their heavyweight in to teach him a lesson. Then he felt a tug again, turned, and there was MacWilliam, throwing off his gloves.

"He was huge, and if I was going to break *anything* on him, it would be his hand on my head." But B.J. never backed down from a fight, so he threw off his gloves and proceeded to get the shit beat out of him. And as B.J. was sitting dazed and seeing stars in the penalty box, MacWilliam yelled over to him, "That's round one asshole!"

The next day in practice, head coach John Van Boxmeer skated up behind B.J. and hooked a hockey stick around his midsection. "How much do you weigh when you're a hockey player?" he asked him. Van Boxmeer already knew it was substantially less than B.J. weighed at the time. "I had a big dinner last night," B.J. quipped, realizing it wasn't an excuse that Van Boxmeer would buy, or an answer he'd find any humor in.

"Okay, well have a nice long drive back to San Diego," the coach told him. But even though he sent B.J. packing, Van

Boxmeer respected his play and go with MacWilliam enough to call him back up to play for the Ice Dogs on several occasions in the next few years.

B.J.'s best friend, and Gull teammate, Darren Perkins, was an exceptional athlete, and a great hockey player. He'd won so many championship rings, he got to know people at the company that made them, and was offered a job when he retired from the ice. And like so many other players, Darren's retirement was decided by an injury.

After twelve years of professional hockey, and during his fifth season as a San Diego Gull, Darren experienced a string of wicked battle wounds all in a single season. The first one came early in the year, when he got slashed in the hand. He felt quite a sting, and as he kept skating, he took off his glove, kind of shook it a little, and his pinky finger fell out onto the ice. His finger had been chopped off by the dull blade of a hockey stick! Luckily, team doctors were able to reattach it.

Darren's quickness and intuitive presence on the ice made him a difficult target to put a solid hit on, and earned him league "Defenseman of the Year" titles on several occasions. But a week or so after recovering from his severed finger injury, the odds caught up to him, and he got checked into the boards so hard his clavicle snapped. He recovered from that injury as well in time to play the later part of the season.

Then, in one of the last games of the same year, B.J. and Darren were on the ice together, playing the Tacoma Sabercats. Tacoma was on a penalty kill, and Kim Maier, a player known for the velocity of his slapshots, launched the puck, putting everything he had into it. Maier's frozen missile hit Darren just below the eye, and B.J. recalls, "He dropped like a sack of potatoes." The puck shattered his nose into seven pieces and eye socket in three.

Focused on covering an opposing player, Darren never saw it coming.

It was one of the nastiest things B.J. remembers ever seeing, and as he was looking down at him, Darren asked, "How does it look? Is it bad?" B.J. just cringed. Darren was hoping for a more positive response. There was so much swelling they had to wait three days to take X-rays. Darren took the third serious injury in a row as a hint that maybe it was time to hang up the skates. And so he did.

Most hockey injuries aren't life threatening, but many are just plain ugly. When B.J. was playing for the Toledo Storm, they had a five-hour bus ride to the old milling village of Johnstown, Pennsylvania. The fifty-year-old arena where the Chiefs played was smack dab in the middle of nowhere. B.J.'s teammate Rick Corriveau caught a puck square in the mouth, and starting spitting teeth out onto the ice. "Chiclets" as they say in hockey.

At least eight came out, and 16 or so were damaged in total. The worst thing for Rick was there wasn't anything anybody could for him out there in the boonies, so he had to get back on the bus for five hours and bear it. His mouth was so sensitive and sore, he couldn't even open it as the air itself was enough to cause him excruciating pain.

B.J.'s good friend Clark Polglase, a former San Diego Gull, also fell victim to a slapshot, but this one hit him in the ear. He was playing for the Bakersfield Condors at the time. It took 100 stitches to sew up the gash, but they didn't do X-rays. The next night he showed up at the game to watch, and his coach said in a bitter voice, "What, you're not going on the ice?"

"That's not a tough coach, that's an asshole," B.J. insists.

Clark was traded about two weeks later. After finishing out the season complaining of headaches, a re-examination found he had been playing the whole time with a concussion and skull fracture they failed to find during the initial treatment. That was Clark's last season, like B.J., Darren and Clark and countless others would have loved to continue to play.

Unfortunately, the very things you love about the game... the velocity of a well-hit slapshot, a perfectly-timed check of an opponent against the boards, a sudden three-on-one opening the opportunity to score a goal, may also end your career in a flash, and long before you want it to be over.

Of course this may happen in any field of work, but in hockey, it's different. For some players, it may end like any other job, as simple and gentle as receiving a pink slip in an envelope, or them deciding they're too old or too tired to do this kind of work anymore. But for too many others, the last day of work ends as abruptly as being kicked down a flight of stairs. At least Darren and Clark were able to walk away. B.J. didn't have that luxury. He would have been thankful for a *limp*.

Chapter 7 - "Don't Pray for Me"

The Gulls won game 5. Idaho Steelhead fans took up a collection and raised more than $4,000 for B.J., a gesture he greatly appreciated, and above and beyond respectful for an opposing team to do. He also had lots of visitors, including players, coaches, the media, and even Boise Mayor H. Brent Coles stopped in to see how he was doing. That's a city that cares, and also a testament to B.J.'s stature as a player.

Angela saw Borzecki in the hallway of the hospital crying. B.J. says he doesn't remember, but she recalls Borzecki going into the hospital room, and B.J. telling him not to worry about the hit... that he didn't think it was done on purpose. B.J.'s version is that Borzecki showed up twice, expressed much remorse, but was denied entry into his room. In a press conference, B.J. told reporters he held no grudge, and he understood it must be a tough thing for Borzecki to come to terms with.

At that point in time, B.J. hadn't seen the game tape yet, which no one would let him watch until weeks later. After he saw it, he changed his mind. It's not that he thought Borzecki meant to end his career in hockey, or permanently injure him, but he felt it was a cheap shot nonetheless. Considering the consequences, it was a difficult act to forgive.

B.J. had only spoken to Steelhead coach John Olver briefly when he coached the WCHL all-star team he was on in the season of 1999-2000. Steve Martinson was assistant coach, and as mentioned, they had never been real fond of each other. So when Olver came to the hospital to see B.J., he wasn't too comfortable with him showing up. "He was a man I barely knew, and the first thing he asks is if I had Jesus in my heart. A strange question from a hockey coach. And then he said I should pray. I told him I don't pray. I believe in God, but I don't like the fact most people pray only when they want or need something, and don't when everything's going their way. Praying doesn't win games, and won't get you out of a hospital bed."

B.J. was adamant about being prepared to take his chances with doing it on his own.

And it's easy to be bitter after a dirty hit just took the one thing you love most in life away from you, not to mention the ability to move your body.

Another day a priest came breezing into the room, looked at B.J. with a Mr. Rogers smile, and stuck out his hand for him to shake. B.J. just scowled at him, "Does it really look like I'm able to shake your fucking hand?" The priest put his hand on B.J.'s, an act that pissed off the incapacitated hockey player even more. "Then he recited a verse, ending with 'John 3:16,' or something like that."

B.J. responded, "'Don't let the door hit you in the ass on the way out,' B.J. MacPherson, 5:15" (that's what time it was).

B.J. admits he was a bit frustrated at the time. But that's a comment that could have easily come from the sassy player when he was healthy and in top form, a virile, quick-witted wiseass who would speak his mind to anyone he felt was behaving inappropriately. His retort showed there was still some fire left burning in him, and that he was determined to fight his way out of this mess. Or at least give it his best try.

While the feisty Canadian wrestled with his paralysis, the Gulls won the next game in Idaho, and were now up three games to two. All they had to do was win one of two games played on their home ice. While it sounded like they were in the driver's seat, the truth is they lost their first two games at home, and despite their impressive Taylor Cup record, had never won a championship series in a home game.

B.J.'s always felt at an advantage at away games. Although it's great to have the support of your fans at a home game, "when you're out there on the ice, you don't notice what's going on in the stands so much." In B.J.'s opinion, it's less comfortable playing away, and this creates a higher intensity for the visiting team and gives them a stronger drive to win. "We always seemed to relax less and play harder when traveling."

It sounds strange, especially when we're used to hearing "home field," or "home ice advantage" all the time, but this series was a great example. The Gulls lost the first two at home, and won the next three in Idaho's arena. Now the Gulls had a good shot of winning it, but returning to San Diego had B.J. a bit nervous. It definitely wasn't in the bag yet, and since the level of his morale and stability of mindset was deeply influenced by the outcome of the games and series, and his recovery hinged on how well he handled his condition psychologically, he felt anxious and skeptical.

Maybe it was purely superstition. Perhaps it was irrational thinking prompted by his crippling injury and all the madness his confinement in the hospital brought him.

But in his mind, the Gulls *had* to win that series, or he was done.

Olver and the Steelheads may have been praying for a couple of wins to snatch the series, but all B.J. could feel is that there was lots of hard work to do, for both him, and his teammates, and somehow his life was at stake. "I may have been a cripple, but I was still captain of the team. And as I told Olver, I don't pray."

Chapter 8 - Mind Games

Two days after his surgery B.J. woke up in a different room. "When did you bring me in here?" he asked. "It's the same room," they told him. A reduced dosage of his medication and he was actually becoming more coherent. Perhaps in his mind he had made a move, the "new room" a metaphor for a different attitude towards his condition. Or maybe those drugs had really done their job.

Still hazy and lethargic, he refused to just lie there in a lump. B.J. began a routine that he would continue for weeks. Lacking any ability to physically move, he decided to *mentally* move each muscle in his body. Since his mind was the only thing really working, he imagined he could work his body parts, and went through a series of exercises, extending and contracting his muscles.

He began with the toes on his left foot, curling them back and forth. Then the entire foot itself, then his ankle, calf, and knee, until he worked up to imagining the whole leg lifting. Then he'd begin with the right leg, starting with the toes, and moving up… ankle, calf, knee, leg. After his legs, he'd start with the fingers on his left hand, doing the wrist, working up the arm, and so on. He'd then do the same with his right hand and arm. *Always* in the same order.

The exercise had a comforting feel to it. Perhaps it was nostalgia, like, "this feels good because this is how I used to move." Or maybe it was hope: "If I envision hard enough my arms and legs moving, maybe I'll eventually get them to do it." That's kind of what he felt. Whatever it was, it felt good, and he promised himself to keep at it.

Put this book down for a moment, lie on the couch or your bed or the floor, and try not to move for ten minutes. You can't roll over, reposition yourself, wiggle your fingers or toes, or lift your arms. No movement at all. Hard to do isn't it? Now imagine being stuck this way. You want to move something, *anything*, but you can't. Although physically it's probably not as much of a challenge, but mentally, and psychologically, it's enough to drive you insane. At least that's the effect it was beginning to have on B.J.

Just like breathing, we don't think about moving our limbs. You have an itch, and your mind sends a message to your hand so fast to scratch it that you're not even conscious of doing it. It just happens. It's automatic. B.J. had to think really hard about every transfer from mind to muscle.

One day in the hospital he had an itch on his nose. Momentarily forgetting about his condition, he instinctively sent an order down to his hand to relieve it, tried with all his might to bring a finger up to scratch, and there was no response. "Get up there and scratch, you bastard!" Nothing. It was driving him crazy, so he started a garbled attempt at yelling for Angela or anyone to come help him out. "I couldn't even scratch an itch on my own fucking nose!"

A nurse came running in, put her ear close to his mouth, and he told her he had an itch on his nose. "From my screams I think she thought I was dying!" She itched his nose for him, and from that day on, every time she sat down with him, she playfully scratched his nose. It became a little joke between them, but the night it happened, he was horrified. Above everything else, not being able to simply relieve an itch hammered home the severity of his condition. B.J. wept all night.

His teammates were now back in San Diego, and had a couple of days off before the next game. It was his third day in the hospital. He did his visualization exercises, and once he was done, his mind raced off into other thoughts. The words of the first doctor continued to haunt him.

"You're never going to walk again, son."

Lots of people came in and out of the room, but he felt alone and trapped inside himself. His mood bounced back and forth from hopeful to dismal…

"I'm a cripple. I'm never going to skate again. I won't even be able to walk. I won't even be able to scratch my nose!"

"I'm going to recover. Play hockey again. They'll see. All those people who think I'm done. I'm going to make it out of this."

"No I'm not! I'm through! Never gonna fuckin' walk! Call Fred. Tell him to come down and pull all of these tubes out of my body, and use one of them to strangle me! Better yet, just do it myself. That's it, I'll kill *myself*… but, fuck! How the hell would I do that? I can't move! I'm so pathetic, I couldn't even kill myself if I wanted to."

"You can do it. You *have* to. A little at a time. Practice. Set some goals. Don't let anyone tell you can't do it. Especially some stupid doctor. Zimmerman's in charge now. The other guy's gone. Zimmerman's gonna get you through this. And Angela, my mom, Darren, Louise, Peggy Ann, Fred, Sandy, Archie… my teammates, friends, the fans… they're all pulling for me. I'm *gonna* be okay."

The conflicted athlete with a petrified torso went back and forth like this over and over, his eyes the only vehicle left to express his sensibilities and pain. A minute felt like an hour, an hour like a day, and all he could do was just lie there thinking, with a giant tube stuffed down the throat of his useless, already atrophying body.

B.J.'s mom knew what he was going through, and although she made it a point to never allow him see her tears, he knew when she had been crying in the hallway by the way her eyes were puffed up when she returned. But Peg's resolve was as solid as his. "Don't you quit boy," she'd tell him frequently, looking him in the eye with the combination of a glaring sternness and deep love only a mother of her character could project at the same time.

"Don't you quit!"

And despite the psychological hell he was going through, he had no intention to.

A doctor he hadn't seen before came in the room nonchalantly and unannounced. A nurse was with him, and she was holding a stop clock. He asked B.J. how he was doing, and then got right down to business.

"Okay, here's the deal son," the doctor began. "We're gonna pull that trach out of your throat and you're gonna have 30 seconds to breathe on your own. If you can't, you're pretty much done... We'll be breathing for you and it's doubtful you'll ever walk again. Ready? "

"No, no!" B.J. gurgled out as much as he could muster those words with the hose in his throat. "Can't we do it tomorrow?" he pleaded. Suddenly the fate of his recovery was staring him right in the eye, and it had the face of a clock! He didn't want to deal with this, wasn't prepared, and was scared to death. He tried to convince them it wasn't a good time, but they calmed him down, and got on with it.

"The doctor pulls the trach out and I couldn't believe how far down into me the tube went. Still in shock about what's going on, I'm looking at the clock, trying with all my energy to breathe, and nothing's happening. Ten seconds go by. There it is again. 'Never going to walk again.' Forget skating, but even worse, 'Never going to breathe on my own again.'"

"Twelve seconds. Nothing." B.J. stares wide-eyed at the doctor and nurse. Fifteen seconds. Thinking about breathing. *"Take a breath or you're through son. We'll be breathing for ya."*

Sixteen seconds, seventeen seconds, he's watching the clock. Trying to breathe with every ounce of energy he has… "Fuck! I'm through! I'm never gonna make it!"

And then, at eighteen seconds, B.J. takes the deepest and most gratifying breath in his life. Before he could even exhale, tears poured out of his eyes. He was getting real good at crying, but this time it was out of happiness, "because it was the first thing I did that they didn't think I could do. And all I wanted was a drink of water, because I hadn't had one in three days." And then he smiled after a little puff of air pushed out of his lungs, carrying his relief.

Now at least he had his mouth back, and he called Angela, his mom, Darren and Louise into the room and proceeded to talk for hours. He had no idea this event was going to take place, but after it happened it felt like a landmark to him. He had a renewed faith in his recovery. He had taken the first step… breathing on his own. For some reason he had a feeling inside the next day would bring something even better.

Chapter 9 - "I Hope We Lose"

During his visualization exercises the next day, a couple of fingers on his left hand moved. Like a child, he excitedly called his family and friends into the room, intent on showing them what he could do. Then he wasn't sure if *he* moved them, or they moved on their own, because when he tried it again, nothing happened. He was tired. The trach removing incident had drained him of what little energy he had.

He slept a good part of the day, continued wrestling with his carnival of thoughts, talked to the media a bit, but couldn't stop thinking about his fingers. He felt sure he could do it again, so he told everyone to be there the next morning, after he had rested. Sure enough, the next day he was able to move the same two, and even a couple of more fingers on his left hand. But then he couldn't do it again. At least he confirmed he moved them himself.

Imagine completely exhausting all of your day's energy just curling your fingers! But that activity alone was enough to consume everything B.J. had in him. That and of course his sharp, racing mind, always in motion, feeding his hope and plotting his recovery. And he felt his strength was building.

B.J. became very excited when it was time to go to sleep that night, because he was sure in the morning he'd have enough energy to do it again. The next morning he was able to move all of the fingers on his left hand, and his left foot as well.

Now his thoughts were setting the pace for his recovery, well ahead of his body. He couldn't wait to go to sleep at night because he thought maybe the next morning he'd be able to move something else. Of course, he wasn't sure if anything else was going to move, and had to repeatedly push the ugly thought out of his head that his progress would stop at some point, perhaps even somewhere far short of walking.

A few fingers moving, or all of them for that matter, wouldn't be much good without the arm working. Ditto for a single moving foot without a functioning leg. But his hope ran wild, and he began making a plan.

The Gulls were playing game 6 that night in San Diego, and if they won, that would be the series. As much as he felt he needed them to win the championship, he actually wanted them to *lose* this game, so it would go to the seventh. His mind may have been working, but nobody could claim it was sane. His plan was for the Gulls to lose game 6, and for the first time in their history, win it on home ice in game 7.

And he was going to be there to watch it happen!

He discussed his idea with the doctors, his family, friends, and team. For the first time since he was carted off the ice, he made people laugh instead of cry.

"You're not going anywhere. You're here for at least three weeks. But it's good to hear you've got some life back in you," the doctors assured him. But those who didn't already know, soon found out just how stubborn and resolute B.J. could be.

His mind was set, and sure enough, the Gulls lost game six of the series.

Chapter 10 - "Can't let You Go"

Of all the teams in the WCHL, the Gulls and Steelheads were perhaps the best funded. This of course, has an impact on the players' morale, and arguably, their performance. Certainly the added resources that result from a team with some money behind it helps. The Gulls' success on the ice was strengthened by a solid team of some of the best staff in the business.

Equipment Manager Matt Mitchell meticulously cared for the player's gear, had a keen sense of knowing what back-up supply was necessary to quickly replace anything that was worn, damaged, or easily broken, and an ample budget to fulfill his "whatever you need" approach to the players. Not all minor pro teams enjoy such a level of care, or are fortunate enough to have such a conscientious, dedicated person minding their gear.

Head Athletic Trainer Billy Taylor also worked with an exceptional commitment to his job and welfare of the team. A former top athlete himself, Taylor excelled as a defensive back for the San Diego State University Aztecs, and was drafted by the New England Patriots. Billy came from good athletic stock, as his dad played for the Brooklyn Dodgers. His dedication and good judgment won the appreciation of the team. "He was respected by the players like no other trainer I've ever known," B.J. said.

In addition to his care of the Gulls, Head Team Physician Dr. E. Lee Rice, is an internationally-recognized authority on sports medicine, a clinical professor at the University of California, San Diego, School of Medicine, the Western University of Health Sciences, and San Diego State University. Dr. Rice has also served as team physician for the San Diego Chargers, the USA Men's Olympic Volleyball Team, and numerous other professional, Olympic and university teams.

In B.J.'s opinion, the level of play and dedication of the team is also a direct result of the owner's involvement. Four Taylor Cup appearances and three wins in the first four years of the WCHL is a testament to Gulls owner Ron Hahn's commitment.

He also owns the San Diego Sports Arena (now, of course the Valley View Casino Center), the Gulls' home rink, and a venue that has hosted such historic events as Ken Norton beating Muhammad Ali to become the heavyweight-boxing champion of the world, and Eamonn Coughlan breaking the world record for the indoor mile on two separate occasions.

Thirty-six years old at the time of B.J.'s injury, the 15,000+-seat Sports Arena (12,920 for hockey) had a long history of professional hockey, hosting its first game (the Western Hockey League's Gulls) on November 17, 1966, the day it opened as the San Diego International Sports Center. The arena has also been home to the San Diego Rockets and San Diego Clippers, both former NBA teams, the 10-time major indoor soccer champions, the Sockers, and indoor football team San Diego Riptide.

Jimi Hendrix, the Doors, INXS, Janis Joplin, the Grateful Dead, Led Zeppelin, the Rolling Stones, Bob Marley, the Moody Blues, Van Morrison, Pavarotti, Pink Floyd, REM, Queen, Nirvana, Frank Sinatra, Yes, the Who, Bruce Springsteen, ELO, Simon & Garfunkel, Crosby, Stills, Nash & Young, Frank Zappa, Creedence Clearwater Revival, and scores of other artists have played at the Sports Arena. Even Elvis Presley played here in 1970, sending a brand new Cadillac back to an arena employee he befriended during his stay for the show.

When it came to the Gulls, Ron was always a behind-the-scenes kind of guy. But when B.J.'s injury occurred, he saw him more times in a month than he had in the previous five years he played for the team. His wife, Linda, even took the time to take B.J.'s mom out to lunch for Mexican food, and Peg fell in love with the chicken quesadilla.

"I owe a lot to Ron, and he really went out of his way for me, doing things he didn't have to do." Not only did he visit B.J. on a regular basis, but on the day of game 7, he paid for his flight on a Medevac from Idaho to San Diego. B.J.'s doctors in Idaho weren't thrilled about the idea, and told him the altitude could seriously threaten his health, if not kill him.

But his mind was set, and he had to go. His mom flew with him, and Angela and Darren took a commercial flight. B.J. was "encased in some sort of human cocoon," flown to Lindbergh Field, and transported by ambulance to Alvarado Hospital, where he was greeted by a couple of photographers. B.J. was pissed off to see them there. His move was supposed to be kept secret, and he really didn't want anyone seeing him in that condition. Except, of course, his teammates. He didn't care how beat up he was, he had some talking to do with them.

As soon as he arrived at Alvarado, the persuasive, driven hockey player began lobbying to go to the Sports Arena. All he cared about was going to the game, and no one was going to stop him. Or so he thought. Gulls team physician Dr. Rice was there, and Billy Taylor was too. They met with hospital administrators on his behalf, and the decision came back.

"I'm sorry," a doctor told him. "There's no way you're leaving the hospital. It's way too risky in your condition, and we can't let you go."

His heart sunk. He had planned the whole thing out. B.J. was in San Diego, just miles from the arena where game 7 was to be played, and they wouldn't release him from the hospital.

"You don't know him," Dr. Rice chimed in. "If he wants to go, he's going."

"But we can't be responsible for what happens," they said. "He's barely out of intensive care. He can't go."

B.J. was so desperate and upset, he even made a silly childish threat. "If you don't let me go, I'm never going to get better!" Yeah, that would show them. It didn't work.

"So you're telling us he's stuck here?" his mom asked.

Dr. Rice took the other physicians aside. Understanding the importance of this game to B.J.'s morale, and recovery, he asked them to find a way to make it happen.

"The only way he can go is if he's signs *himself* out." They continued, "But we don't recommend it..."

"Where's the paper?" B.J.'s mom demanded.

And then she grabs B.J.'s limp hands, squeezes both of them around a pen, and puts a big "X" on the release papers where the signature's supposed to go. Peg understood too. This was closure for B.J., the last game of his career as a player. He *had* to be there. His was still the guy with the "C" on his sweater, even though he wouldn't be suiting up. Marty confirmed this with him, and as ragged as he was, every one close to B.J. understood the meaning of this championship to his life.

Ron Hahn came through again, and had an ambulance there for him. Since he was officially signed out of the hospital, none of their staff was allowed to help get him on the stretcher. The guys who came for him didn't really know what to do, or how to lift him.

That's when B.J.'s newfound buddy Thor the nurse came through. A big guy with a blonde flat top and muscles on top of muscles, Thor picked B.J. up single-handedly and got him on the stretcher. As an employee of the hospital, he wasn't supposed to help, but he knew B.J.'s story, and realized how important it was for him to make it to the game.

With Angela at his side, they made their way to the Sports Arena. Slightly oblivious to the severity of his condition, or what this day meant to B.J., the drivers expressed their excitement about getting into a championship hockey game for free.

Once at the Sports Arena, B.J. was transferred to a wheelchair, but nobody could figure out how to get him secured to it. So they fastened his legs to the support bars with hockey tape. It was the first time he sat up since his injury occurred, a position his doctors feared he wouldn't fare well in.

He was wheeled directly into the locker room. B.J. asked everyone to leave but his teammates. This was still *his* team, he was its captain, and he proceeded to chide the players. The night before he was listening to the game on the radio, hoping they would lose.

Now he was criticizing them for how they played! And from a wheelchair no less. He said a few things some players didn't like, but he figured they wouldn't dare try to hit a paralyzed guy taped to a wheelchair. Turns out he was wrong about that.

Still feeling they held his fate in their hands, B.J. peppered them with a team captain's scolding. Sure he wanted them to lose the night before, but he'd be damned if they were going to lose tonight! He told them nobody's bigger than the team. As much as he wanted them to win for him, the important thing was to win it for themselves, for the *team*. They deserved it. Earned it. But it was going to take a lot of hard work, he told them.

And then he said, "This is how hard you're going to have to work," and he wiggled his right foot, and lifted his left foot higher than he ever thought he could. It was the most movement he'd achieved since he was hurt, the most he could squeeze out of the limited energy and muscle mass he had, but enough, he had hoped, to get them inspired. He wanted to show them he was going to be okay, and that they should focus on the game. "I guess it worked, because they all jumped up and started charging out of the room."

Some of the players couldn't even look him in the eye, and he couldn't blame them, as he was pretty rough looking... Emaciated, stiff, pale, bleary-eyed, and stitched up incisions on both sides of his neck. He was a horror movie zombie after a nasty car wreck. But to others, he was the same player before leaving the ice in game 4, their teammate and captain, and in the excitement they had forgotten he had a spinal injury, because as they were running out of the locker room they were all rapping him on the head!

"I was yelling, 'Hey, guys, I'm still fucked up! Be careful!' But they were too pumped up to realize they were hitting a guy with a broken neck in the head!"

They wheeled him up to a special platform in the Zamboni door, with a tent around it to maintain his privacy. His friend Clark stood next to him, and put his hand on B.J.'s without uttering a word. They watched the game like that, in silence, for what seemed to B.J. to be a considerable length of time. The Gulls were in top form, and B.J. had never seen them play better. But he couldn't watch for long. His doctors were right. The sitting up was taking a toll on him. He was sweating profusely; burning up so bad they had to start cutting his clothes off.

His ambulance drivers were so caught up in the excitement of watching the game, Angela had to remind them that B.J. was still in their care. They took his blood pressure, and it was dropping so fast everyone started getting worried. He lost vision in his right eye. His system wasn't working so well to begin with, and now it was shutting down fast. And the game was only about eight minutes into the first period.

Once they lied him down on a stretcher he felt better, and had just enough energy left to talk to the press for a few minutes. But then he realized he was seriously pushing his luck. He had to get back to the hospital. Angela rode with him once again, and despite being in excruciating pain, his mind remained fixed on the game.

Like his health at this point, it could have gone either way. He had already recovered more than he was expected to.

But did he foolishly waste his last burst of energy on a life-threatening trip to the Sports Arena? Did he do more damage than good? Would the boys pull it through?

Too much excitement for one day. He was exhausted, as was Angela, and they both fell asleep in the hospital room as the Gulls battled the Steelheads on the ice.

Chapter 11 - Hockey under the Palms

Besides the fact that Ron Hahn's Gulls were treated exceptionally well by the fine organization he'd established, there's another element to explain their success. Great players. And how does the team get them? Well, the weather certainly doesn't hurt. Who wouldn't want to finish hockey practice and enjoy 70° temperatures on a January afternoon? Maybe hit the beach for a little while or bike the boardwalk.

San Diego was an easy sell, and combined with the professionalism of the franchise, a great fan base with one of the best attendance records in the league, and the team's history of winning, players in minor pro hockey have not only begged to play here, some have actually taken pay cuts just to stay.

When the San Diego Gulls began playing in 1966, construction of the San Diego International Sports Center had yet to be completed. They played 13 games on the road in the Western Hockey League waiting for the rink to open, and on November 17, beat the Seattle Totems 4-1 in their first home game. With chicken wire for glass, visiting teams were heckled by the Gulls infamously rowdy fans, and the arena was filled with them, with crowds often exceeding 10,000.

This was rough and tumble old-style hockey, with lots of brawls, run and gun style of play, no helmets, sparse padding, and more lenient rules than present day leagues. One Gulls fan recalls the Portland Buckaroos' Connie Madigan getting a few beers thrown on him through the chicken wire in a playoff game, and just moments later, punching out a referee, dropping him to the ice.

Back in the days when Gordie Howe was still grinding it out for the Detroit Red Wings, it's hard to imagine the game in full swing under the sunny skies of San Diego. But years later, Mr. Hockey himself would actually play in the Sports Arena.

The Gulls had eight seasons in the WHL, before it folded in 1974. Led by the great Willie O'Ree, who was not only the first Gull to ever have his number retired, but also the Jackie Robinson of professional hockey when he became the first African Canadian or African American man to play in the NHL as a Boston Bruin in the season of 1960-61. (O'Ree is African Canadian.) Ross Perkins, Darren's dad, was also on that team, which made the playoffs every season except the first, but failed to win a Patrick Cup.

The World Hockey Association's (WHA) Jersey Knights relocated to San Diego and then became the Mariners, playing at the Sports Arena the following three seasons. The WHA was formed in 1972 to compete with the NHL, and lasted until 1979, when the two leagues merged. The Mariners played nineteen teams in their last two seasons in the WHA, including four teams which were absorbed into the NHL: the New England Whalers, Winnipeg Jets, Edmonton Oilers, and Québec Nordiques.

Although it seems an unlikely place to own a place in the history of hockey, San Diego and the Sports Arena had many legends grace its ice. Gordie Howe, playing with his son Mark on the Houston Aeros, unleashed some of his magic here against the Mariners. So did Bobby Hull playing for the Winnipeg Jets, and Frank Mahovlich playing for the Toronto Toros. And even Gretzky was a San Diego Gull from 1991 through 1993. Not Wayne, but his brother Keith, who played his last two seasons here before going on to coaching.

For the 1977-78 season, the Mariners played in the Pacific Hockey League (PHL). The following year the San Diego Hawks, also of the PHL, called the Sports Arena home, and from 1990 to 1995, the Gulls returned as an International Hockey

League franchise. The Gulls of the IHL included Steve Martinson and Denny Lambert, who would go on to play six full seasons in the NHL.

The Taylor Cup, played the best of seven, began as the championship series with the formation of the West Coast Hockey League in 1995. The Gulls won the first three years, under the leadership of Martinson, who had 434 wins under his belt as a coach of the team and a winning percentage of .714; one of the best in all of professional hockey. Marty had also been the Gulls general manager for seven of his nine years with the team. An NCAA all-star, he played professional hockey for 14 years, including 49 games in the NHL.

The year the Gulls began in the West Coast Hockey League, B.J. was with the Toledo Storm, playing alongside future Gulls teammates Mark Stitt and Dennis Purdie.

B.J. joined San Diego for the season of 1996-97. They had a great team, and won the Taylor Cup in a four game sweep of the Anchorage Aces. The Gulls beat the Fresno Falcons to win the cup the year before as well. B.J.'s teammates included Darren, Clark and the Gulls' legendary enforcer, Chad Wagner, as well as Martin (St. Amour), his brother Stephane (both of whom had over 100 points each that year), and Mark Stitt and Kevin St. Jacques (who both also broke the 100 point mark).

Brad Belland was a standout, and Taj Melson worked hard and played exceptionally well too. Former New York Ranger star Ron Duguay played two full seasons with the IHL Gulls, and joined B.J.'s Gulls for a few games in 1995-96, 1996-97 and 1997-98.

"Duguay showed up for games in his vintage Rolls Royce, sometimes with supermodel wife Kim Alexis. He insisted on sharpening his own skates, and when his line went on the ice, he'd go full bore at about 100 miles an hour for 30 seconds or so, then come right off. He was fast as hell out there."

Extremely diet and nutrition conscious, Ron was always lecturing. "You shouldn't eat dairy products," he once said to B.J. during practice. "But what would I pour over my Fruit Loops and Cocoa Puffs Ron?" he toyed with him.

While some of B.J.'s teammates became good friends, others were simply guys he worked with. Some he liked, some he didn't. But he put that all aside when on the ice. One player he wasn't very fond of, and never said a word to after games and practice, had a presence on the ice that meshed very well with B.J.'s, and they played great together. Others were the complete opposite.

"Brad Belland was great with his stick, and always felt more comfortable when he was handling the puck. We hadn't been on the ice together before, and the first time we went out on the same shift, we skated right into each other and both ended up on our backs. On the bench, we looked at each other and laughed. We couldn't be on the same line. We both liked having the puck too much!"

And good players know their role, and where they fit. Not everyone gets recognition from the fans, but the best guys don't care about that so much. They're doing whatever they can for the win, for the team. The fan favorites are important to keep attendance up. Every crowd knows at least three players: the team's top goal scorer, their best fighter, and the goalie. The goalie's role is clear, the enforcer's misunderstood but always a darling of fans when the gloves come off, and it's obvious what the goal scoring finesse player does best.

B.J. explained emphatically, "What many fans don't see is how the players work together on the ice, and how every great scoring line has a bartender and a mucker, as well as a goal scorer. While the mucker sets the pick, screens the goalie, or takes a defender out of the play, the bartender feeds the goal scorer who takes the shot."

B.J. was the mucker on his line. This doesn't mean he received less credit than he deserved, or he was any more or less important than anyone else. He had a role to play, a job to do, and he knew his place. And he was comfortable in his position. The important thing was to win games, and it took team play to do that.

"I was one of nine picks the year the Washington Capitals drafted me. The late, legendary Jack Button, Washington's chief scout and director of player personnel, took us all out to dinner one night. He went around the table and pointed to each player. 'You're going to win the Hart Memorial Trophy,' he said to one of the draftees. 'You're going to win the Lady Byng award,' he said to the European player. 'You're going to get the Art Ross Trophy,' he said to another.

He went through every player at the table and named every award possible to receive for outstanding play in the NHL. He finally got to me, and said, 'B.J., you're not ever going to win an award…but you're going to be the glue that holds a team together.' In B.J.'s mind, Button couldn't have paid him a better compliment.

In addition to playing center for the Gulls, being a mucker, and having the honor of wearing the captain's "C" on his uniform for three years, B.J. also did various other things to show his loyalty to the team. While playing, he was signed for one game as coach, unofficially assistant coached, sold tickets, helped with marketing and promotion, and even drove the team bus, assuming the wheel from Coach Martinson.

B.J. recounts the event, which occurred just a few months before his injury… "Marty didn't normally drive the bus either, but after playing in Fresno one Saturday night, we had to get to San Diego for a game the following afternoon. Our driver was lying on the floor when we began to board. 'I can't drive,' he said. 'Too sick.' Marty starts growling at him with his raspy voice like the kid's a player, 'Suck it up, c'mon, we have to go tonight, right now. C'mon, toughen up, let's go, get up.'"

"'Can't do it,' the driver says, so Marty tells him to sit close by, and our coach proceeds to pull the bus out of the parking lot as the driver tells him what to do. He has us on the highway, and not more than ten minutes later, calls back for me. 'B.J.!' he yells, and like an echo all my teammates follow. 'B.J., B.J., B.J.! Marty wants you up front.' I knew what he wanted, and was excited. I had always wanted to drive the bus, and lots of times after games I'd sit in the driver's seat. 'C'mon,' I'd say. 'Let me take it for a while.' And then the driver would reply, 'Get out of here. You can't drive this bus. Go sit down.'
I never did get to try. Now I finally had my chance."

"'Okay,' Marty says, 'This is what's gonna happen. I'm gonna slide out of the driver's seat, you're going to be holding the wheel, and then you're going to slide in.'"

"'Uh, okay, Marty. But aren't we going to pull over first?' We were speeding down the freeway. "

"'No. We're not pulling over. No time. Ready to take it?' So he slides out, I slide in, and now I'm driving the bus. The real driver, looking twice as sick as before we left the parking lot, and for good reason, is sitting there watching and whimpering like a puppy dog."

"As we proceed down the highway, he whispers tips in a faint, mousey voice… 'Don't get too close to that guy in front; it takes a while to stop. Let some air out of the brakes. Keep both hands on the wheel,' etc. It was comical. I guess he said, 'Pull the bus over first and stop before you switch drivers' too softly for Marty to hear."

Funnier yet was the view behind him. "If you've ever been on a team bus after a hockey game, you know it's a scene right out of a war movie." Bodies strewn everywhere, guys passed out in strange positions, sleeping in the aisles, anyone still awake bleary-eyed, nodding out, and looking half-dead.

Once B.J. took the wheel, it was a different story. Marty's mid-highway transfer served to perk them up a bit, and now they sat upright, alert and wide-eyed, *all of them*, and watched in a semi-horror they would never admit as someone who had never driven a bus before suddenly held their lives in his hands. And wore a shit-eating grin as he was doing it no less.

"I'm sure I'm the only one who enjoyed *that* ride," B.J. beamed. But I got us there, and even backed her right into the Sports Arena parking spot and tooted the horn a couple of times to announce our arrival."

Sure B.J. had always wanted to drive the bus, but even if he *hadn't* wanted to, he would have done it if it were necessary for the team. And this wasn't the only time Marty tested B.J.'s level of commitment. Just as hell-bent on winning as B.J. was, Martinson tirelessly hounded the refs during games when a questionable call was made. And he did this through his captain, repeatedly sending him out to pass along comments and inquiries about the practicality of their judgment.

In the heat of one battle, Marty sent B.J. after the ref to pose this question: "What the fuck? B.J., you go ask that guy if he's reffing a badminton game or a volleyball game!" Having been directed to challenge the ref a few times before, B.J. knew the question he was asked to deliver wasn't going to help Marty's already tentative standing with the ref much.

"Uh, I don't think I should really tell you what Marty wanted me to say," B.J. tells the official.

Then the ref responds, "Well you tell *him* if he doesn't shut-up he's gonna be looking at a penalty."

B.J. goes back to the bench as Marty waits impatiently for the reply.

"Well, what did that asshole say," he asks B.J.

"He said 'a badminton game,'" B.J. reports.

"Yeah, that's what I thought," Marty replies.

~

It seemed to B.J. like Angela and he had only been asleep for a few minutes when the phone rang, but in fact they had both been completely conked out for hours.

The game had been played, the series was over, and the locker room was exploding in celebration on the other end of the line. Gulls 4, Idaho 1! The Gulls won the Taylor Cup! Seven games, home ice, perhaps the most important win of B.J.'s life. The victory sent his emotions soaring. Hockey may have ruined his spine, but at least he knew the team had his back. It may have even overtaken being drafted by the Capitals as the best day in his life.

Or maybe not…

Chapter 12 - Reality Check

The morning after the Gulls won the cup proved to be one of B.J.'s worst. Hockey season ended, just like it had for him every year for the past twelve. But this time was different. He knew his teammates were out partying in celebration all night, and they wouldn't even be hung over in the morning because they were too pumped up. Of course he wanted to join them, but was stuck in bed.

Besides the fact that B.J. loved partying almost as much as he did playing hockey, that wasn't the worst part. He lay there knowing his career as a hockey player was officially over. Winning the championship or not, the end of the season was always a letdown to him, but then, "before you knew it, the next one started."

The end to this particular season gave him the hollowest feeling in his stomach he's ever felt. He really *wanted* to feel good, celebrate the victory the only way he could, in his thoughts, but the feeling didn't last.

He looked down at his limp body. He could barely move his left hand and his legs. He couldn't eat or go to the bathroom on his own. He couldn't even control his own bowels, couldn't turn himself over, change his position, or get out of bed. "I still couldn't scratch my fucking nose."

The day before, winning the championship meant everything to him. When reality pulled him back into bed, he felt like the win meant nothing. It was bad enough hockey was over for him permanently. What the hell was he going to do the rest of his life, when all he ever knew how to do was skate and now he couldn't even walk?

He had made tremendous progress, both physically and mentally. But he was still a heap on a hospital bed, and compared to before his injury, had almost no muscle left at all. What little physique he had left barely functioned. The same qualities that got him this far along in his recovery - stubbornness, determination, and a perpetual hatred of losing *any* challenge were a double-edged sword. His physical progress fell far behind his will, and dealing with his own impatience became a challenge in itself.

As much as he appreciated Martin St. Amour's support, he even began refusing to see him. One day he came in and B.J. had made some progress, the next day he came in he wanted to show him he could move something else, but he couldn't.

Initially, it appeared movement was coming pretty fast, but it proved to be only a spurt during the last few games of the championship series. B.J. remembers showing Martin how he could move his leg, and the next day he came in and said, "Okay B.J., what can you move today?" Of course he meant well, but when B.J. couldn't move anything different the next day, he felt like shit. So the next time Martin showed up, B.J. told the nurse not to let him in.

His emotions swung back and forth so fast, at times he even surprised himself. He'd be talking to one of his friends that came to see him, saying "Yeah, I'm feeling better, I'm gonna get through this okay."

A minute later, when no one was in the room, he'd be in a ball crying and the nurse would come in asking if he wanted to see so and so.

"No! I can't," he'd say, sobbing. "Don't let them in!" The next time the nurse would come in he'd scowl at her, "I hate you! Get the fuck out of here!" Then he'd feel totally hopeless, "like I just wanted to give up and die. I finally just refused to let *anyone* in."

One particularly depressing moment came when B.J. found himself in front of the mirror for the first time since the injury happened. He was in the bathroom down the hall from his room, had his shirt off, and couldn't believe the skeleton he was seeing before him.

"I looked like a POW." From a superiorly fit 210 pounds, he had dropped 50, nearly one quarter of his entire body weight, and almost all muscle. He was literally just skin and bones.

Chapter 13 - Baby Steps

One day a hospital staff member came bouncing down the hall. He was friendly, enthusiastic, and had the best intentions for B.J.

"Okay B.J., I have here the Cadillac of wheelchairs for you!"

A spectacular piece of equipment, with controls and all sorts of gadgets for someone in his condition to operate it. B.J. asked the guy to come near the bed, and then he spit at him. "Fuck you! That's giving up! Get that fucking thing outta here!"

B.J. later confessed he felt bad about his behavior. But all along during his time in the hospital, he refused such devices, such as the TV remote control designed to be operated with one's mouth and teeth. It was the principle that made him scoff at these things.

If he accepted a special wheelchair designed for someone with almost no mobility, he'd be accepting his injury and a limited recovery. In his mind, he'd be giving up. B.J.'s rationale was that if he sat in that thing today, he might be sitting in it five years later as well. And that was a prospect he just couldn't accept.

The first few days of B.J.'s physical therapy consisted of a couple of nurses coming into his room, putting a series of braces on him, getting him dressed, moving him to a different bed, sitting him up at a 45 degree angle, and watching his blood pressure until it fell too low for him to continue.

Once he was able to handle the pressure of being upright a little better, they repeated the same procedure of bracing and dressing him, wheeled him down to the rehab room, had him do some very basic extension exercises with his left arm and leg, then

71

wheel him back. It took half an hour just to get him ready. The process took all of his energy, and he'd crash for a couple of hours before lunch, and the next session in the afternoon.

As much as it drained him, and was a daily reminder of how little physical activity he could actually do, he lived for these sessions, and watched impatiently for the clock to hit nine every morning. Since that was the time they set for his session, he was pissed off when they were late. "I felt as if my rehabilitation would be delayed days or weeks for every second they came after our scheduled time. And I wanted to get out of there as soon as possible."

In the mornings before physio, he went through his visualized movement exercises. He could actually move his left hand, arm, and foot. While his therapists worked on that side, his right side wasn't showing much sign of improvement. His visualizations of it moving helped him cope psychologically with his immobile side.

Psychiatrists on the other hand, did not. B.J. never wanted to talk to them. Nothing personal, but he didn't feel like telling his problems to a stranger. "Get the fuck out of here," he'd yell in his characteristically diplomatic fashion every time they tried to enter his room.

But B.J. pushed himself throughout his physical therapy. If they wanted him to do ten reps curling his arm, he'd do fifteen. From the time he entered the hospital, he felt like he'd always proved them wrong. Though realizing their intentions were good, he took every bit of bad news or doubt about his condition as a direct challenge he wasn't about to back down from.

When they thought he couldn't breathe on his own, he did. When they told him he couldn't handle going to the game, he went. So when they gave him an exercise to do, he'd try to exceed the repetitions, even double them if he could muster the strength.

He was beating the odds originally given to him when he arrived in such a sorry state. Soon he would face the biggest challenge, and the words continued haunting him… "Never going to walk again." Fuck you. Challenge accepted, but he wanted to do more than walk. He wanted to skate.

His progress continued. He was feeling stronger. B.J. was able to stand upright, but only with the help of the physio staff holding him. The local press, following his recovery, celebrated B.J.'s ability to take a few steps, but the therapists were actually doing it for him. With braces on his legs and bands attached to the braces, they moved his legs in stepping motion, like he was a giant human puppet.

He had many different physical therapists, and liked most of them. But Matt was the best. The physio center they always took him to was on the same floor as his room, and he always had several people working with him.

And then one day, Matt took him to a room on another floor. This time, it was just B.J. and Matt, and he helped him to the parallel bars. "What do you think, want to go for it?" the physical therapist asked. "What, try to walk?" B.J. replied quizzically. "Yeah," Matt said. "Think you can do it?"

And then B.J. tried, and took the first two steps on his own. Matt was excited, and encouraged him to take a few more, but B.J. was done for the day. That was enough. It was another breakthrough for him, but he wasn't hooting and hollering or anything like that. They took him downstairs, and B.J. told his mom he took a few steps. She was excited, so the next day B.J. had her and a few other people in the room, but he didn't do as well, as he was too pumped up and wanted to show everyone what he could do so badly, he burned most of his energy before he even got there.

He found his worst days in physio always came after his emotions skyrocketed the night before. This time he simply used so much energy thinking about walking the next day, he had none left to do it. "Some nights I was such a wreck emotionally, I was toast the next day. But the first steps were another landmark for me, and I had erased another doubt. I could walk on my own."

B.J. pushed himself every day, and took more and more steps. Never without the help of the support bars, but he knew that day would come as well. It was just a matter of time. Physically he was progressing more quickly than anyone had thought possible, but in his mind it wasn't fast enough.

"I wanted it to happen more rapidly than it was taking. I got impatient. I continued wrestling with the thought that I would hit a wall. Maybe I really couldn't walk without the use of those bars propping me up. Maybe my left side, the stronger one, would come back completely, but the right one would remain limp forever."

Chapter 14 - Six to Eight

Physio was the best part of his day, but also the most frustrating. They had him do things like lie on a mat and try to roll himself over, move some skateboard like things on a table with his arms, and push himself off of a wall while standing against it. Such basic movements, yet sometimes he still couldn't muster the energy or coordination it took to do them. His right side wasn't working.

The nights back in bed after therapy were brutal. Since he couldn't pee without the use of a catheter, they had to use one on him several times a day. And as if that wasn't uncomfortable enough, one night he lied there and his penis began stinging. "It felt like it was on fire!" The result of a bladder infection caused by an unsterile catheter, B.J. says "It was easily the worst pain I've ever felt in my life. I screamed for the nurse, and she turned me over and gave me a shot.

"Good night," she said, thinking whatever she injected me with would be enough to put me right out. She was wrong. Twenty minutes later, still wide awake and yelling in pain, I called her back in. I didn't have too many nice things to say to her, and she flipped me over and gave me another shot. 'Now, GOOD NIGHT!' she said again, in an annoyed voice.

Another twenty minutes later, still wide awake and totally pissed off at this point, I yelled again. 'HEY! GET THE FUCK BACK IN HERE! IT DIDN'T WORK!'"

With B.J.'s dick still burning out of control, a doctor came in, and looked at his chart. He seemed confused a double dose of the sedative the nurse had administered had no effect on him. They flipped him over again. This time they gave him an Opium suppository. Ten minutes later, he nodded out with a smile on his face and was drooling on himself.

B.J. always crashed after physio. The morning one wasn't so bad, because he knew after lunch he'd have another. But after napping from the afternoon session, he dreaded waking up and dealing with the night. From six p.m. to eight p.m., he was always at his worst. Angela was still at work and his mom had left for the day, so neither was there at this time. He was left in bed, in the dark, with only his thoughts and partially functioning body.

After about three weeks in the hospital, he decided he had enough. It was around 6:30 p.m. Now able to roll himself out of bed and into the wheelchair, he fumbled into it, and with his left arm and left leg, pushed himself all the way to the elevator at the end of the hall.

He was so slumped down in the chair, he made it under the nurses station window without them seeing him. When he got to the elevator, he couldn't get his arm up high enough to push the button. So he just sat facing the elevator door, slumped over, looking at the button from the corner of an eye in his sideways head.

That button was his freedom.

He was thinking about how he could push it, how nice it would be to be back in his own home, how he wished he could just get up and walk right out of that building, maybe go to the arena, put on some skates, shoot a few pucks… But all he could do was sit there. A minute or so passed.

The elevator door opened, and he figured luck was with him. He looked up, and there was his nurse. "Hi B.J. Going somewhere?"

76

She asked in a tone as if speaking to a small child. And he felt like one.

"Yeah. I'm outta here. I'm going home, " he replied.

"Hmmmm. Going home huh? That's nice. How are you going to get there?"

His head dropped down, and his eyes were looking at the floor, as if he were a kid who had just gotten caught by his mother doing something he knew he wasn't supposed to do. "I'm gonna take a taxi," he mumbled.

"A taxi huh?" Her voice was a mix of pity and humor. He realized she wasn't going to let him leave, and started sobbing.

"Do you have any money to pay for the taxi?" she continued.

As if that were the only reason he couldn't go, he whimpered, tears now dripping on the floor. "No, I don't have the money." She turned him around and pushed him back to his room.

Chapter 15 - Club Med

After physio sessions, B.J. would look forward to his medications and crashing for a couple of hours. They'd wheel him past the nursing station and he'd announce "twenty-two!" His code for the two Percodans and two Somas they owed him after his workout.

He ate, took his pills, and quickly fell asleep looking forward to the next session, which he was determined to make better than the previous one. His medication not only helped him rest and regain the energy required for rehabilitation, it helped soften the aches and pains, both physically, and psychologically, he was dealing with.

One of the worst nights in the hospital came when B.J. was sedated in the afternoon, but a shift change and oversight lead to a missed evening dosage. When the medication wore off in the middle of the night, B.J. awoke feeling the full extent of his injuries in a raging nightmare he was fully conscious for. He screamed in agony and was quickly assisted, but not before the realization of his plight imprinted in his mind and gave him anxiety for the next few days.

And the thought of never playing hockey again was the most haunting of all to B.J. He wrestled with this likelihood as he worked to regain movement in his body. Progress was happening more quickly than physicians had foreseen, and B.J. kept up at proving everyone wrong. His performance at rehab sessions was steadily improving. And he even began getting his spunk and sometimes perverse sense of humor back, much to the chagrin of the U.S. Marines.

A young, injured marine was brought to a room on B.J.'s floor one day. Sometime after he arrived, his family came and took him without anyone knowing, sparking an AWOL investigation that had military police charging through the hallways of Alvarado. Shortly after his evening dose of meds, B.J. admitted he was feeling loopy, and the soldiers poked into his room.

"Anyone in here?" they asked. And B.J. replied, "Just me!"

Then he asked one of the nurses what the commotion was all about, and the next time he heard the boots of the MPs clacking down the hall, he decided to tip them off. "HE'S IN HERE! HE'S IN HERE! HE'S IN HERE!" B.J. yelled to them. When the uniformed men came racing into the room, rifles slung across their shoulders, they shouted excitedly at B.J., "Okay, where is he?"

To which B.J. replied, "HE'S UNDER THE BED!"

Of course, the young soldier wasn't under the bed, and had never been in the room, but to B.J., and the pills he was under the influence of, this was very funny, and he laughed as the marines scoured his surroundings. "Not funny sir," they told him, and as if that wasn't enough to satiate a need for entertainment that had been starved for weeks, B.J. yelled again minutes later as he heard the men returning from searching another section of the hospital floor.

"HE'S IN HERE!" B.J. yelled again, and when the soldiers came back and asked where, B.J. replied, "HE WENT OUT THE WINDOW!" Seeing the windows didn't open enough to allow a grown man out, the marines scolded B.J., who couldn't hold in his laughter. An armed soldier was placed at B.J.'s door as the others continued their search.

A bit more unexpected entertainment came from B.J.'s first physio trip to a local YMCA pool. Rehab staff would bring B.J. and other wheelchair bound patients to the facility in a van and place them in the pool using a special lift. The water allowed patients a broader range of movement, and the buoyancy made it possible for B.J. to stand upright in the water, something he could not yet do on dry land.

Wobbling, he had all of his weight on the left foot, and used the tippy toe of his right solely for balance. Angela had accompanied B.J. to the Y, but wasn't in the pool. He worked his way over to her. For weeks B.J. had been unable to urinate without the help of a catheter. Now standing in the pool, he had what was to him at the time a very strange sensation.

He whispers to her, "Hey Angela, feels like I could pee. What should I do?"

With a group of firemen working out on bikes and treadmills behind the glass on a split-level just above the pool looking down at him, Angela whispers back, "It's okay, it's a pool. Go ahead and pee in the water!"

So after a little straining, B.J. says, "I don't know if I'm doing it..."

"You are, you are!" Angela returns. "Start splashing around the water!"

"What do you mean?" And then he looks down and sees the problem.

Tremendously gratifying, the first piss on his own. The only hitch was his system had so much medication in it, his pee came out purple! They both watched as the brightly colored cloud appeared around him. And as he tried to move the water around with the only hand that worked, his left, he lost his balance and started to fall backward into the water. Trying to keep his head out of his own pee, he bobbed forward, then lost his balance again and bobbed back. Angela was cracking up, and B.J. was laughing so hard and trying to stay upright at the same time he was trying not to drown in the purple water. When he looked up, the firemen were laughing too.

And then he felt embarrassed. It was time to go back to the hospital room for some more meds and sleep.

Chapter 16 - "Get Me Out of this Laundry Basket!"

B.J. still had a long way to go. But the progress kept coming slowly. Physicians anticipated him being in Alvarado for two to three months, but he was determined get out of there faster than that. And twenty-four days after he returned to San Diego, and thirty-one after he was first injured, he left the hospital for home. Even though his doctors thought it was too soon, B.J. felt it was time to go.

With tensor bands on his legs, and a frailty that could actually allow a strong enough puff of wind to knock him over, B.J. could now walk on his own in a stiff, awkward Frankenstein-like manner. Getting out of Alvarado was a milestone to him, as were things most would consider too menial to measure, like taking the first dump on his own, which he accomplished the first day home.

He was in the hands of Angela, his mom, Darren, and others who cared about him. In addition to paying for her apartment while B.J. was in the hospital, Ron Hahn had made arrangements so his mom only had to pick-up the phone, call Cloud 9 Shuttle, tell them her name, and a car arrived shortly thereafter. What Ron did for him provided tons of inspiration that B.J. considers critical to his recovery.

Being home presented a new set of challenges. While he could roll out of bed into a sitting position, and walk around ungracefully, he still only had 50 percent or so of his original mobility. His right side lagged far behind his left, so his strong side had to help his weak side do things. "Many things I just couldn't do. Like get dressed or open a jar of food. I couldn't even get up off the couch."

The first day back in Point Loma, he, Angela and Darren went to the El Torito restaurant across the street from his apartment. He ordered a coke, and was too weak to pick it up with his left hand. His right hand didn't even work.

Bending over to drink through the straw proved to be his only option, and although it was a dilemma physical in nature, it made him feel mentally retarded. Fifteen minutes later, he lost all of his energy, slumped over and was unable to continue sitting at the table, so they had to get the food to go and return home.

Despite his condition, B.J. fought to bring some normalcy back into his life. A few days later his friends Clark and his boss Scotty Wright, General Manager of Marvin K. Brown used cars, picked B.J. and Angela up in a full-sized Cadillac to go see a Padres game at Qualcomm Stadium. It was a comfortable ride to the game, and B.J. was excited to get out of the house and do something. Tim Hudson was on the mound for the Oakland A's, but shortly thereafter unintentionally ruined the experience for B.J.

"I never forget the game because of Hudson. He must take longer in between pitches than any other pitcher in the league. I was thinking he was an asshole because he was so slow, I only lasted two innings." Just sitting in a stadium seat took so much out of B.J., he had trouble walking out of the place, but refused to ask for a wheelchair.

His emotions continued to swing in a multitude of directions. He was glad to be home, but had less help than when in the hospital. He still couldn't dress himself, and the first few weeks fell more often trying to get around in his apartment than he had in all his years on the ice.

Getting up after a fall presented an additional challenge, especially if no one was there to help. "I took some good fucking spills in the apartment. And they were always worse when nobody was around." He wanted to get out of the house and do things, but he didn't want anyone to see him in this condition. And the nights were particularly bad, when he didn't have extra medication to help soften the anxiety, aches, and pains.

The rate of recovery in his mind continued to exceed his actual physical progression, and he often got himself into difficult situations. Going to the bathroom was always a big challenge, and as a result of his injury's impact to his nervous system and basic functions, he had trouble holding it in when nature called.

One day on the way home from having far too many beers he should have had at Lahaina, a popular watering hole just off the sand in Pacific Beach, he told Gulls Equipment Manager Matt Mitchell to immediately pull the car over. When he opened the door, B.J. fell out. Matt picked him up, helped him over to some bushes, and had to hold him upright while he peed on the side of the road.

"I've probably taken a hundred pisses in public, not something I'm proud of, but it was either that or pissing myself." After Matt dropped him off at his condo, B.J. took a couple of steps up the stairs in the front of the building, lost his balance, and fell right on top of a small, newly planted tree, uprooting and flattening it in the process.

B.J. was so fragile at the time, he could have easily broken a bone or two on any given fall. But a bit of luck was on his side, and not one of them caused further injury. One day, walking through his bedroom, B.J. lost his balance and fell right into a laundry basket, with the laundry cushioning his fall. Unable to get himself out, he remained there flustered until his mom finally heard him yelling. For months these kinds of situations occurred.

While some of the stories are funny now, imagine the frustration he felt going from a professional athlete with the balance to fly down the ice on a couple of thin blades of stainless steel, to a half-functioning human who could easily topple after tripping on a pebble or nothing at all, lacking the strength or mobility it takes to get back up.

The physical challenges wore away at his mental state, and he hovered on a fine edge between determination and hopelessness, optimism and depression.

At the dinner table one night, about a week after he got home, his mother watched him struggling to hold a fork in his hand and become frustrated enough to pick the food up with his fingers. She decided at that moment it was time for her to go back to Canada. She realized he was at a point that any more of her help would have slowed down his rate of recovery, rather than benefit it.

As tough as it was for her to go, and to watch him struggle, in her mind, it was the best thing she could do for him… Allow B.J. to re-build his strength by doing more and more things without her help. As she had done before when he was an adolescent, Peg knew the same tact was required now. She decided it was time to send B.J. back out into the world to fight…

Chapter 17 - A Hockey Game Broke Out

Fighting isn't merely a metaphor for the determination B.J. has shown in his attempts at recovery. It's a critical component of hockey, in his opinion. Often criticized, even by such legendary players as Wayne Gretzky, and the subject of much controversy, the topic prompts followers of the game into long debate about whether fights belong in an era gone by or should continue to be a part of modern-day play.

Ironically, the year The Great One was honored with *Sports Illustrated's* Sportsman of the Year Award - arguably due to his efforts towards minimizing fighting in the NHL as well as his record-shattering performances on the ice – and on the night the magazine's staff was there to give him the award, he got into a fight with Neal Broten. One of the few of his career, but it happens.

Critics may claim hockey fights are arbitrary violence, but in B.J.'s view, play a critical role in the strategy and outcome of the game, as well as in the business of the sport. The days of players in the NHL recruited solely as "goons" or "enforcers," however, are gone.

Everyone in the league must now be able to contribute something other than being good with his fists. Although being a decent fighter is definitely an asset, players must now possess the speed, strength, stamina, and superior hockey skills to make an NHL team. The reason for this is simple. A player with poor hockey skills, who is purely on the ice to fight, will purposely be left unchallenged by the opposing team. That'll give them a one-player advantage, sort of like a free power play.

Since the minor professional teams are required to have a quota of rookies, and often a substantial one at that (the ECHL, for example, at the time of this writing, allowed only four veterans out of the 20 active players on a team), you'll see more fighting. In addition to strategy, the rookies fight to show their dedication to the team, and also to establish themselves.

Those who feel fighting is a valuable component of hockey, which can help win games, and even championships, frequently point to the Philadelphia Flyers success in the seventies. The Flyers won the Stanley Cup in the seasons of 1973-74 and 1974-75. They not only outscored their opponents, (with their division-leading 273 goals and 112 points in 1973-74, and 293 goals and 113 points in1974-75), but they outfought them as well, leading the entire league both years with 1,750 penalty minutes in the first year they won the cup, and 1,969 the second.

Well-known as the "Broad Street Bullies," their style of play was exceptionally rough, and this, backed by the skills required to protect their own net and put the puck in their opponent's, proved to be a winning combination.

The Gulls won more Taylor Cups than any other team in the WCHL, and lead in penalty minutes every year since it was formed in 1995.

As Gretzky has said, "hockey is a game of finesse." But it's also a game of intimidation. It requires speed, strength, skill, and toughness, and at times in no particular order of importance. But toughness frequently supersedes the rest.

Players are often on the ice fatigued and hurt, get hit on a regular basis, and eventually get called out to fight by an opponent, slashed in a place pads don't cover, or receive a cheap shot that rattles the bones. They get the hell beat out of them, and continue playing on pure adrenaline, because often that's all they have left.

Some players don't fight, and that's fine, but every team needs at least one watchdog, and you can bet the other team's going to have one as well. And the emphasis here is on "team." Fights may appear to just be between two people, but the players out there punching away are always doing it for the team. B.J. recalls Steve Martinson yelling at any players sitting on the bench during a fight. "Stand up and cheer him on! He's out there fighting for *you!*"

When Brian Morrison was playing for the Gulls, he was the epitome of a team player, a true gamer. He wasn't the Gulls' fighter, but one night he went up against the Tacoma Sabercat's enforcer. The first blow he took sent him down to one knee, but he got up and kept swinging. Once the refs broke it up, he skated directly off the ice.

None of the Gulls' knew why until they got into the locker room, and saw his jaw bandaged up. One of the very first few punches he took broke his jaw in two places and pushed his front bottom teeth halfway down his throat, yet he got up after that and kept fighting.

A fight like that can really perk up a team when their play is flat. A strategically timed fight can also change the tempo of a game, tame a cocky opponent who's getting a little too loose with his stick, keep cheap shots to a minimum, or simply bring the tone of play up a notch.

There's never been a great quarterback in football without a good line in front of him. And could a passer ever achieve greatness if his front men let the rushers through? The same holds true for hockey. Finesse players can do their scoring more easily with protection.

Of course some players, like Gordie Howe, could score *and* fight. But players like this are the exception. Most of the best scorers focus on getting the puck down the ice and into the net, and are much better at doing so when they know there's someone watching their back. By nature, hockey players are tough, but even the brawniest ones think twice about continuing to harass a top goal scorer after that team's 6'5," 250 pound enforcer just knocked a couple of his teeth out.

And the truth is, more players skate away from fights unharmed than those who get injured. Those fans that dislike fighting in hockey are often not familiar enough with the game to know its role, or realize that it actually keeps the game safer. A controlled fight with bare fists prevents aggression from being carried out in other forms, such as with the clubs hockey players carry in their hands and the knives they wear on their feet.

New rules heavily penalize instigating fights, so a player who goes at another without that players consent, is simply wasting penalty minutes for his team. In minor pro, players often agree to fight each other before they throw the gloves down, and the best enforcers are smart fighters. They know when to do it at strategic times in the game, benefiting their team, and without having to be told by their coach.

Lots of players will be called out by another to fight, and flatly turn down the offer. Many times a visiting team player won't drop the gloves with an opponent in an away game, but invite the same guy to fight when he's on his home ice. And then that guy may refuse! This sort of thing would make Martinson's blood boil, and B.J.'s too.

One player who never refused a fight was the Gulls all-time best enforcer, and one of B.J.'s best friends, Chad Wagner. At 6'4," 245 pounds, he was formidable enough, but the size of the fight inside of him was bigger than the frame that held it. He's the only player B.J. knew who would lose a fight, and get excited about going at it with the same guy again. Not that he'd lose too often. One year he had 521 penalty minutes… just a bit less than some entire teams in the WCHL had in total for all of their players combined!

After so many fights, Chad developed a crowd pleasing post-brawl routine that included playing air guitar and shooting imaginary guns into the air.

Chad liked to fight, and he was good at it. And interestingly, like many of hockey's great fighters, he was funny too. He had lots of lines he'd say to players considering going a few rounds with him. "You want five to ten," (holding up his right hand), or "life?" (holding up his left). If someone was eyeing him, he'd say, "What's wrong, am I wearing something of yours?" And to a young player who was trying to prove himself by fighting him, "You gotta work your way up to a title shot kid before you try me."

Some may think players like Chad are barbarians, but what they don't realize is they're just doing their job. Absent an enforcer on a minor pro team, its opponents may wreak havoc on their players, preventing finesse play and dominating the ice.

Enter a tough guy on the team that had none, and the playing field is leveled. Fights have a purpose in hockey, and sometimes help win games. And just as many enforcers in hockey, like Chad, have a surprisingly good sense of humor and wit, many of them have hearts as big as their biceps.

Chad would be the first one down at the shelter on Thanksgiving serving turkey meals to the homeless, and he helped start the Gulls "Toys for Tots" drive. Still going to this day, the program collects and delivers toys and games for underprivileged children throughout San Diego County.

Not to discredit the true love of hockey in all of its forms by its many fans, but the reality is, for every fan that's in the arena to watch a hockey game, there's at least one other who's there to see the dukes come out. And there's nothing wrong with this. After all, people go to boxing bouts to see a fight.

Most don't want to see someone seriously injured, but enjoy the physical contact, as pure a competition between two athletes can get. The scrapping is an important part of hockey, and whether someone is there to appreciate every aspect of the game, or has solely come to see a fight, collectively they make up the fan base, pay the large salaries of players, and help the sport to thrive professionally.

Chapter 18 - Back (Down) on the Ice

For weeks after the accident B.J. had a reoccurring dream. It was more like a single image imbedded in his mind, which came to him most often while sleeping, but sometimes even when he was awake. Steel rafters crisscrossed high above him, flickering lights, and he couldn't figure out what they were, or why he kept seeing them. A creepy silence and maze of metal that he couldn't shake from his thoughts.

Then one day, he finally realized what he was seeing... It was the ceiling at the Bank of America Centre in Boise, Idaho. It was what he was looking at the exact moment his hockey career ended. The image was as cold and frozen in his mind as the ice he was lying on the last few minutes he was a hockey player.

When I first got to know B.J., I remember thinking how great it must be for someone like him to have known from the time he was five years old exactly what he wanted to do in life. Long into adulthood, his mind hadn't changed. To him, there simply *wasn't* anything else.

He loved hockey, he wanted to spend his life playing it as often as he could, and he was fortunate enough to have had the opportunity to make a nice living doing it. What could possibly be better, knowing without a doubt, almost from birth, precisely what you wanted to do in life? No going from one dead-end job to another, changing careers, switching majors in school, wracking your brain trying to figure out how the hell you're going to pay the bills doing something at least mildly stimulating or enjoyable to you.

For B.J., this challenge had been painlessly worked out long before the word "career" even entered his adolescent vocabulary. He wanted to play hockey, he was good at it, and he was paid to do it.

The day his injury occurred, it struck me that there was a down side to that bliss. I hadn't even thought about it before. What if suddenly you couldn't do that thing? The only work you've ever known and loved to do? Then what? That's the prospect B.J. faced as he was being taken from the ice. From that moment on, heaven in a hockey uniform turned to hell in a hospital bed, and B.J. stared from a wrecked body into the haunting abyss of his own future.

He continued physical therapy three days a week at Alvarado Hospital's San Diego Rehabilitation Institute. Cloud 9 Shuttle picked him up and delivered him home after each session. B.J. couldn't drive, and tired of the lack of freedom he had from relying on others to transport him around.

Finally, he couldn't stand it, and hobbled down to his truck. With only the use of his left hand, his body hunched over and still half functioning, he drove to Details Hair Salon where Angela worked in Ocean Beach. B.J. had to use his knees to help him make right hand turns. But he got there. Whether Angela or his physical trainers were more upset was a toss-up, but he was sternly reprimanded by all of them, the keys were promptly taken away from him, and he had to undergo special testing at rehab the next day.

Month after month, B.J. continued his efforts at regaining the functions he had as a man and a professional athlete. Rehab, pisses in public, and awkward spills in strange places became part of his routine, but he never lost his commitment to become whole again.

At the Gulls home opener the following season, he joined his teammates to celebrate the Taylor Cup. He was supposed to just touch the 40-pound trophy as it was lifted during the pre-game ceremony at the Sports Arena. The banner commemorating the team's championship was dropped, players gathered around the Cup, and B.J. surprised everyone by hoisting it into the air, using his left hand to do the work and dummying his right to get it over his head.

He went to practices and sat in the stands. Continued his physio and pushed himself harder than therapists asked of him. At a baseball game in October, he challenged a couple of guys who were picking on a small African American man. "Pretty tough eh? How about a go with me?" When a scrap ensued and B.J.'s clumsy left-handed swings caused him to lose his balance and fall, Angela jumped into the fight. "He's got a fucking broken neck!" She yelled at them. But B.J. was on the mend, both physically and mentally.

In November of 2001, the Gulls recognized B.J.'s contribution to the team by retiring his number, an honor that has only gone to two players before him.

Doctors told him the extent of his progression was limited, but through determination and hard work, he consistently proved them wrong. Eight months after his injury occurred, B.J. was confident enough about his physical condition to put on skates.

Nervously, he stepped on the ice, took a few steps, and fell flat on his face, knocking himself unconscious.

Chapter 19 - Number 28

B.J. continued going to Gulls' practices, and stayed in touch with the game through contact with his teammates and coaches. An excellent public speaker, able to capture the hearts and imaginations of others with his colorful, inspirational talks, he became a member of Sharp Healthcare's "Sharp on Survival" team.

Lecturing to business associations, spinal injury patients, and children with incurable diseases, B.J.'s remarkable journey and gift for storytelling mesmerized audiences, made them laugh, and even made them cry. The Gulls organization recognized his speaking abilities and gave him a job as a color analyst, alongside veteran broadcaster Chris Ello for all televised games on Channel 4 San Diego.

B.J. finally felt ready to prove to his fans he was serious about the mark he had set for his rehabilitation. Saturday night, March 8, 2003, before the Gulls took on the Fresno Falcons, he prepared for the mother of all his appearances as a speaker and hockey player.

In front of a crowd of 9,332, on "B.J. MacPherson Night" at the Sports Arena, attendees watched a compelling video chronicling his career, injury and fight for recovery. Then, as part of the "Sharp on Survival" program, he spoke for nearly half an hour, recounting the madness he endured as a result of the blow he received in Idaho.

As if standing there upright on his own in high spirits wasn't amazing enough, B.J. took to the ice on skates and circled the arena, hockey stick in hand. In addition to ending his career with a standing ovation on home ice, B.J. left as the franchise's second all-time leading scorer with 345 points, third in all-time goals with 137, second in all-time assists with 208, fifth in penalty minutes with 699, second in games played with 309, and second in plus-minus at +163. B.J. was going out a winner. But his stats pale in comparison to the level of inspiration he left teammates and fans...

Get your head rammed into your spine, take a few punches when you're lying there down on the ice, become paralyzed, have some doctors tell you you'll never walk again, lose the only thing you've ever dreamed of doing and love in life, get tubes shoved down your throat while being told you'll be a vegetable if you can't breathe when they pull them out, cry at night and fight during daylight hours with every ounce of energy left in your emaciated frame, fall in bushes, pee all over the place in public, spend years in therapy, and then, after lacing up the old skates and doing a few laps around the ice for old times sake, laughing about the whole thing as you recount to your friends how fucked up it was. *That's* a hockey player. That's tough. That's B.J. MacPherson.

Afterword

About two months after B.J.'s skate at the Sports Arena, I was at his second annual "I Broke my Fucking Neck" party. The fact that he has such a thing speaks volumes about how he's come to terms with his career-ending injury.

And just as most people wouldn't have a party with such a theme, I think it's safe to say most people who have suffered a crippling spinal cord incident like B.J.'s don't recover as well as he has. Sadly, many remain bedridden or in wheel chairs. Others die, and B.J. was, in fact very close to death on more than one occasion due to his injury, including the night it occurred.

During his rehabilitation there were many times he *wanted* to die, but it was his desire to live that saved him, and the outpouring of love and support he received from family, friends, teammates and fans.

At the party in his condo in Ocean Beach, California, I was drinking a beer and talking to one of my friends when out of the corner of my eye I saw a flash of movement. Someone had just run down the stairs. I turned and found, to my great surprise, it was B.J., and just then it hit me how miraculous his recovery had been. I followed him into the kitchen. "Who's writing your book B.J.?"

"Nobody," he answered.

"Well, I can write as well as you play hockey," the alcohol in my system exaggerated.

He had had some offers. Some he refused and others fell through. We agreed to sit down the following week. For more than two years we met and talked. I took notes, wrote chapters, and we decided on a format B.J. called "like Pulp Fiction," bouncing around all over the place. That took off but didn't fly, so I decided it would be stronger coming directly from B.J.'s perspective. He tells the story, I ghost write it in his words, editing and polishing as we go. This didn't work either, as I failed to capture his voice in a way he felt comfortable with.

More than three years after we first sat down to talk about it, the book still was uncompleted, much to the disappointment of both of us. When the first draft was finally ready in 2006, and a slew of query letters sent, the Gulls folded, leaving a gaping hole in our promotional strategy and promises we couldn't keep to prospective publishers. The book remained unpublished.

From his perspective, it's a difficult story to tell. Not that the words don't flow freely from his mouth... The truth is, he's not only a better hockey player than I am a writer, but he's far more articulate and colorful when speaking than I could ever possibly capture with the written word. Anyone who's heard him commentating a Gull's game, attended one of his spirited talks, or experienced him recounting some of his misadventures the day after at a party can attest to that. B.J. has a natural talent for gab.

It's often uncomfortable for B.J. recounting the tale because it's the story that chronicles the end of a lifelong love affair he had with playing hockey. But it didn't come without positives. It brought him and his beautiful wife Angela together. Got me out of a foolish agreement I made with him that involved me standing on the ice while he shot a puck over my head at 90 miles per hour.

And it gave him an opportunity to participate in other aspects of the game. After doing odd jobs, owning a coffee kiosk, and working construction, B.J. was hired as assistant coach for the Gulls. Upon completion of the first draft of this book, he was

Associate Coach, sharing management with former teammate Jamie Black. After the Gulls folded, B.J. became a successful salesman for a linen rental company, Specialty Textile Services, LLC.

An insightful, intelligent person with loads of common sense, an in-depth, first-hand knowledge of and experience in hockey that players respect, and a personal demeanor comprised of equal parts of toughness and fairness that his team recognizes and responds well to, B.J. has all the makings of a first-rate, successful coach, should he be given that opportunity again.

While he feels he was "kicked out of the game," he definitely fought his way back into it, paid his dues, earned his stripes, and in his characteristic determined fashion, may someday regain a strong presence in hockey, on the other side of the bench or in another area of an organization.

B.J. inadvertently summed up to me how his struggle has influenced him as a man and a coach when he recounted one of his experiences behind the bench. One of B.J.'s players, Nikita Korovkin, was in the corner during a Gulls away game against the Stockton Thunder. Korovkin passed the puck, and had his back towards center ice, when a Thunder player hammered him from behind, head first into the glass.

The young Russian goes down, and has to get his face stitched up by team doctors. The sight of a player getting pounded by a cheap shot drives B.J. crazy, and he starts thinking to himself, "Someone get that fucking guy, someone *has* to get that fucking guy!" As soon as the Stockton player's penalty was up, and after the game had halted for a few minutes for a television timeout, B.J. saw the player was back on the ice.

There he is, he's out there! Who's going to step up? B.J. thought. Gulls forward, Rob Flynn, a recent Harvard graduate who chose

101

the ice over a boardroom, understands the situation, skates out and drops his gloves with the guy.

It wasn't much of a fight at first, with both of them stumbling and half-falling as they swung. But as the Thunder player regained his balance, Flynn one-punches him squarely in the jaw and knocks him out cold.

As he watched, B.J. experienced a wide range of emotions. First, seeing a cheap shot delivered stirred up an ugly ghost and made him livid. Then he wanted revenge on the player. Next he was worried about Flynn getting hurt. After that his heart sunk for the *other* guy when he saw him lying on the ice immobile. And finally, he yelled at one of his own players for cheering after the player Flynn floored was down, unconscious, and not moving.

B.J.'s thought process during this series of exchanges demonstrates a combination of integrity, hockey instinct, passion for the game and familiarity with its unwritten code of conduct, and compassion for the players on the ice battling it out, regardless of whose side they're on.

He feels these things because he's developed into an introspective, self-aware, and intuitive man, without growing soft. Priceless souvenirs collected from being in the exact same place himself.

That night in the kitchen at B.J.'s party, I wondered why I felt so strongly about writing his book.

Then I remembered recounting the events of his mishap and recovery to my family and friends, and finding myself getting so choked up, I was often on the verge of tears, unable to finish. Every time I tried to explain what he went through, what the game meant to him, and the raw, unfettered passion that pumped his blood for a game that could drain it in a few seconds without a second thought… It ate at me, but not necessarily in a bad way. Just why was I so compelled to work on this?

It occurred to me days later as I thought about it some more, and then it finally hit me. It was, plain and simply, a story just too good not to be told.

B.J. MacPherson #28

Season	Team	League	Regular Season						Playoffs				
			GP	G	A	Pts	PIM	+/-	GP	G	A	Pts	PIM
1990-91	Oshawa Generals	OHL	57	8	16	24	77	--	16	3	1	4	25
1991-92	Oshawa Generals	OHL	60	20	32	52	108	--	7	2	5	7	27
1992-93	Oshawa Generals	OHL	57	42	55	97	112	--	13	7	14	21	30
1993-94	Oshawa Generals	OHL	44	33	44	77	76	--	--	--	--	--	--
1993-94	North Bay Centennials	OHL	15	9	21	30	36	--	18	11	20	31	24
1994-95	Greensboro Monarchs	ECHL	15	4	7	11	34	0	--	--	--	--	--
1994-95	Toledo Storm	ECHL	54	16	30	46	117	13	3	1	3	4	18
1994-95	Worcester IceCats	AHL	2	0	0	0	8	-1	--	--	--	--	--
1995-96	Toledo Storm	ECHL	64	22	45	67	251	10	5	1	3	4	10
1995-96	Worcester IceCats	AHL	11	1	1	2	10	-5	--	--	--	--	--
1996-97	San Diego Gulls	WCHL	60	29	47	76	157	--	8	4	8	12	30
1996-97	Long Beach Ice Dogs	IHL	4	0	0	0	7	-1	--	--	--	--	--
1996-97	Las Vegas Thunder	IHL	1	0	0	0	0	-1	--	--	--	--	--
1997-98	San Diego Gulls	WCHL	63	25	50	75	181	--	13	3	6	9	45
1997-98	Long Beach Ice Dogs	IHL	1	1	0	1	2	1	--	--	--	--	--
1998-99	San Diego Gulls	WCHL	61	37	43	80	160	37	12	5	4	9	14
1998-99	Long Beach Ice Dogs	IHL	4	1	2	3	2	2	--	--	--	--	--
1999-00	San Diego Gulls	WCHL	68	22	39	61	94	21	9	5	4	9	14
2000-01	San Diego Gulls	WCHL	57	24	29	53	107	22	10	2	7	9	12

The Internet Hockey Database - www.hockeydb.com

105

2000-2001 WCHL San Diego Gulls

Player		Age	Pos	GP	G	A	Pts	PIM	+/-
Mike Taylor		29	C	72	17	69	86	108	24
Mark Woolf		29	R	67	39	43	82	119	8
B.J. MacPherson		26	C	57	24	29	53	107	22
Jeff Petruic	To Bakersfield	26	L	65	27	22	49	41	17
Dan Gravelle		30	W	69	17	28	45	102	13
Petr Marek		31	C	68	12	29	41	83	18
Brett Larson		28	D	70	8	33	41	42	2
Dennis Purdie		27	R	55	24	13	37	123	-5
Jamie Black		28	C	72	9	28	37	70	17
Mark Stitt		29	C	72	13	18	31	62	-1
Samy Nasreddine		24	D	52	9	21	30	49	21
Taj Melson		26	D	31	6	22	28	47	19
Cory Laylin		30	D	27	9	18	27	20	10
Brian Morrison		26	C	54	10	12	22	81	-1
Chris Johnston	To Colorado	25	L	23	10	5	15	12	1
Ashlee Langdone		20	R	61	7	7	14	367	-6
Tim Lovell		26	C	7	2	8	10	0	3
Serge Visegorodcevs		24	D	34	1	8	9	44	12
Kevin Mackie		21	D	43	1	7	8	54	13
Daniel Shank	From Phoenix	33	R	7	2	4	6	6	2
Serge Crochetiere		20	D	39	2	4	6	75	-5
Martin St. Amour		30	L	14	1	4	5	45	3
Darren Perkins		31	D	17	1	2	3	12	-2
Clark Polglase		31	D	10	1	1	2	32	-1
Steeve Vandal	From Colorado	21	R	11	1	1	2	22	-5
Chad Wagner		25	R	32	0	2	2	217	-1
Trevor Koenig	From Idaho	25	G	41	0	2	2	37	0
Marc Laforge	To Bakersfield	32	D	4	0	1	1	12	-3
Cris Classen		25	G	28	0	1	1	0	0
Sean Halifax		24	D	1	0	0	0	15	0
Mike Correia		24	G	1	0	0	0	0	0
Dmitri Doulebenets	To Colorado	22	D	1	0	0	0	0	-1
Denis Lariviere		20	G	1	0	0	0	0	0
David Brito		21	F	1	0	0	0	0	0
Garret Stroshein		20	W	3	0	0	0	5	-1
Konstantin Simchuk		26	G	15	0	0	0	4	0
Bench		--	--	72	10	0	10	30	0
Totals		--	--	--	**263**	**442**	**705**	**2,043**	--

The Internet Hockey Database - www.hockeydb.com

WCHL San Diego Gulls

Season	GP	W	L	Pts	Coach	Result
1995-96	58	49	7	100	Steve Martinson	**Won Championship**
1996-97	64	50	12	102	" "	**Won Championship**
1997-98	64	53	10	107	" "	**Won Championship**
1998-99	71	45	19	97	" "	Lost in Finals
1999-00	70	46	16	100	" "	Lost in round 2
2000-01	72	50	17	105	" "	**Won Championship**
2001-02	72	47	22	97	" "	Lost in round 2
2002-03	72	45	22	95	" "	**Won Championship**

The Internet Hockey Database - www.hockeydb.com

Made in the USA
San Bernardino, CA
14 April 2018